LIVING *on* ★★★★

How to live with passion, motivation, and joy

HIGHER

~ *A salute to the military life* ~

GROUND

April 28, 2011

Paul Laurence Vann

LIVING on
How to live with passion, motivation, and joy
HIGHER
～ A salute to the military life ～
GROUND

PAUL LAWRENCE VANN

Laurel Wreath Publishing
Fort Washington, Maryland

Living on Higher Ground © 2005 by Paul Lawrence Vann

Published by:
Laurel Wreath Publishing
938 Swan Creek Road E. #144
Fort Washington, MD 20744, U.S.A.
www.paullawrencevann.com

Laurel Wreath Books are available at special quantity discounts for bulk purchases for sales promotions, premiums, fund-raising, or educational use. Special books, or book excerpts, can also be created to fit specific needs. For details, write Laurel Wreath Publishing at address listed above.

Cover design: Dunn + Associates Design
Interior design: Folio Bookworks
Back Cover Copy: Write to Your Market Inc.

Printed in the United States of America

Publisher's Cataloging-in-Publication Data
Vann, Paul Lawrence
Living on higher ground : how to live with passion, motivation, and joy : a salute to the military life / Paul Lawrence Vann — Fort Washington, Md. : Laurel Wreath Publishing, 2005.

   p. ; cm.
   ISBN: 0-9764679-0-9

1. Motivation (Psychology) 2. Goals (Psychology) 3. Inspiration 4. Success. 5. Conduct of life. 6. Families of military personnel — Conduct of life. 7. Families of military personnel — Mental health. I. Title.

BF503.V36 2005
153.8—dc22   0503

Contents

ABOUT THE AUTHOR

Paul Lawrence Vann, Lieutenant Colonel, USAF (Ret), served over twenty years of military duty. He served ten years in the United States Air Force and ten years in the Air National Guard.

Lieutenant Colonel (Ret) Vann was assigned to the Pentagon over twelve consecutive years working for the Air Force, Air National Guard, and National Guard Bureau, which is a tribute to his leadership skills and his value to the armed services. He is a highly decorated military officer who always inspires and motivates others to be the best—either in the enlisted or officer corps—while in uniform serving the United States of America.

In May 2002, Paul Lawrence Vann founded and became President/CEO of Laurel Wreath Communications Inc., a motivational speaking company located in the Washington, DC metropolitan area. Paul retired from active duty in October 2002, and began professional speaking on a part-time basis. He accepted employment with a defense contracting firm and for little over a year worked as a program analyst for Family Programs for the National Guard.

Paul Lawrence Vann's passion for speaking resulted in him leaving to become a full-time professional speaker, and he hasn't looked back. Paul is a professional speaker and professional member of the National Speakers Association.

His publishing company is named Laurel Wreath Publishing. *Living on Higher Ground* is the first of many books which represents a series Paul is writing.

Paul was prompted to write this book because many of his friends serving in the military want to know his secrets to success. Paul Lawrence Vann knows motivation is the key to high morale for our men and women in uniform who put service before self every single day. He also supports and inspires military families and youth because he knows they serve on the homefront before, during, and after their loved ones have deployed to the frontlines in defense of a grateful nation.

Preface
A Note to the Reader

NOW MORE THAN EVER OUR MEN AND WOMEN IN UNIFORM and their families need motivation to sustain them during challenging times. As Americans, we are sensitive to the fact that our country is in the war on terrorism for the long haul. In spite of the challenges, troops from all branches of the military, their families, and all Americans should continue to strive for Living on Higher Ground.

As a Lieutenant Colonel (Ret), I know what it takes to be successful and I take you on a journey to help you achieve even greater success during these challenging times. *Living on Higher Ground* chronicles my life from the time I was born until I retired from the military and became a professional motivational speaker.

I take you behind the scenes and share personal and professional insights about my life and how I went from a life of abject poverty to become an Air Force leader. Readers will not only learn about Paul Lawrence Vann; they will also learn the key events in my life that propelled me to overcome obstacles.

Living on Higher Ground is an inspirational book and a salute to the military life. This book is for family, friends, and the military. I reveal my secrets to success so you can apply some of them to your life and begin Living on Higher Ground.

At the conclusion of each chapter action plans are prepared so you can review the main points and take notes. This book has thirteen chapters, so there is ample opportunity to discover my secrets. You are encouraged to apply these secrets to your life. You will have an opportunity to reflect, meditate, and think about your dreams, goals, and purpose while reading this book.

Don't hesitate to contact me by mail, email, telephone or fax. I look forward to communicating with you in the near future to discover how you are Living on Higher Ground.

Paul Lawrence Vann, Fort Washington

Dedication

I DEDICATE THIS BOOK TO MY MOTHER, MRS. MARTHA Elizabeth Hawkins Vann, and my father, Mr. Edward Cecil Vann, who died before its completion. They live on in my heart and in this book. Simply stated, I would not have written this book without their parental guidance.

Over the course of my life I have never forgotten the love Martha and Cecil shared with me and the character they exhibited as parents. My parents are my role models and they prepared me for Living on Higher Ground because they showed me how to live with passion, motivation, and joy. My parents were the embodiment of two people who lived with a lack of financial resources, yet were able to overcome the odds to prove that spiritual resources are more abundant. Martha and Cecil's vision of what life should be is my reality today.

This book is also dedicated to my wife, Marites, and my daughter, Paula Marie, who I love with all of my heart. My wife and daughter supported me in my quest to write this book because they know how important this message is for families, friends, and the military. Last but not least, I thank all eight of my siblings and their families and all people Living on Higher Ground.

Acknowledgements

In no way have I cited in this text all of the people responsible for this book. I want to thank our leaders who support our nation's armed forces. I thank all of the men and women in uniform who serve our country with distinction and honor— you are our heroes and so are your families. I salute all of our military departments because you know what teamwork really means to our country. Last but not least, I thank our military veterans because they paved the way for freedom, liberty, and hope.

I thank Dottie Walters for the outstanding consultations she provided me. She was instrumental in setting me on my path to professional speaking success in 2002. I thank Kathi Dunn for the superb cover design she developed for this book. Thanks to Write to Your Market, Inc. for writing the copy on the back cover. I also want to thank Liz Tufte of Folio Bookworks for the exceptional interior design work she provided for this book. Thanks to Vera Turner for her book review assistance.

Thanks Jacqueline, Gloria, Eugene, Joan, John, Michael, Cynthia, Dyral, and Tonya for being the best brothers and sisters in the world. A special thank you goes out to Charles Brown, who personifies what a best friend should be—thank you for your invaluable wisdom on life.

I sincerely thank all of these outstanding people. Everyone I mentioned played a pivotal role inspiring and motivating military personnel and their families as they contributed to this work.

～ 1 ～

Martha & Cecil Vann's Son

Paul, you are our oldest son,
and you are a blessing to our family.
—Mrs. Martha Elizabeth Vann

"MARTHA, YOU ARE GOING TO HAVE TO PUSH HARDER, THE baby is almost here! Push girl, push, Lord have mercy Martha, it's a baby boy," said Grandma Annie Bell. Martha said, "Praise the Lord, I have a son." It was 3:00 a.m. on September 4, 1958, as Grandma Annie Bell stood by her oldest child's bedside at Jubilee Hospital in Henderson, North Carolina. The doctor said, "Martha you were in labor for quite a while but you did great, congratulations."

"Cecil, come on in here now, you have a baby boy," said Annie Bell as she walked to the hospital waiting room. Getting up from his seat Cecil rushed to see his new born son. "Look at him, that's my boy," Cecil said with a big smile on his face.

"Let's name him Paul Lawrence," said Carolyn Faye, Martha's youngest sister. Carolyn being a poetry lover had Paul Laurence Dunbar, the African-American poet in mind at the time she came up with her recommendation. Martha's other sister Ruth said, "I like the name because our younger brother who died was named Lawrence, so let's name him Paul Lawrence."

On December 29, 1951, Edward Cecil Vann and Martha Elizabeth Hawkins were married in a small family ceremony. Over six and a half years later, I was born and named Paul

Lawrence Vann. At the time of my birth Martha and Cecil lived in a community called South Henderson. They lived in what is called the "Mobile" section of town. The name for the area where my parents' house was located is affectionately called "The Heights." After several years of saving what little money they earned working at J.P. Taylor's Tobacco Company, Martha and Cecil moved less than a mile away to 340 Skenes Avenue in Henderson, North Carolina.

Families play an important role in the fabric of American society and the role my family played in my childhood was crucial to my success. The Vanns and the majority of their extended family lived in a small rural town named Henderson, North Carolina. Henderson is located nineteen miles south of the Virginia border off Interstate 85, and forty-five miles north of Raleigh, the capital of North Carolina. Henderson, like most small towns in the state, is a part of what is known as Tobacco Road.

My family roots consist of the Vanns and Hawkinses, which represent my mother's side of the family. Both sides of my family lived on the other side of the tracks. Mind you, the other side of the tracks during my formative years didn't denote the wrong side of the tracks, just the side of the tracks where poverty, segregation, lack of opportunity, and racism intersected. Privilege was something my family read about in a book or magazine because our reality was anything but.

My immediate family tree consist of Edward "Cecil" Vann marrying Martha Elizabeth Hawkins. Five years after getting married, my parents had their first child, a girl, and named her Jacqueline. Less than two years later I was born. This is the story of my life from abject poverty to becoming a United States Air Force leader.

"Paul Lawrence, you are our oldest son and a blessing to our family," said Martha. The matriarch had spoken and I said, "Momma why do you say I'm a blessing to our family?" Martha stated, "Because I know you're going to grow up and do great things in this world, I could sense it when you were in my womb." After that single conversation, I set out to discover the world around me and it presented some very amazing challenges, learning that is.

"Son when you were born I was twenty-eight years old and your mother was twenty-five when you were delivered at Jubilee Hospital," Cecil stated. I said, "Dad what was it like when momma was in labor, and I was born at three o'clock in the morning?" "Well son, Martha was in labor for a long time and we knew she was in for the fight of her life delivering you and I always want you to remember when you're faced with challenges you will always be able to overcome them through struggle," my father said.

I will always remember what my father said because being in poverty is the personification of struggle and little did my parents know they would have ten children (my parents lost a son in 1963 during delivery). My brother Eugene was stillborn on the same day President John F. Kennedy was assassinated in Dallas, Texas. I will always wonder what life would have been like had Eugene lived.

My parents had five girls and four boys. I am the oldest son and as my mother stated, "a blessing to our family." Being the oldest son in a Southern family means you will be the leader of your siblings. Make no mistake about it, my oldest sister Jackie and I in many ways raised our younger siblings to help shoulder some of the burdens around the house, so our parents could attend to their jobs and parenting.

My siblings in birth order are Jacqueline, Gloria, Eugene (deceased), Joan & John (twins), Michael, Cynthia, Dyral, and Tonya.

Jackie and I were the only two children for a number of years; however, my parents also became temporary guardians of four of their nieces and nephews for a few years. Steve, Jeff, Sheila, and Ida are my first cousins. Had my parents not taken them into their home, the likelihood is they would have been placed in an orphanage. It's good to know they were able to overcome adversity in their youth.

Neither of my parents graduated from high school; in fact, my mother stopped attending school in the eleventh grade after her father, Phillip Hawkins, died of colon cancer. Unfortunately, my grandfather passed away before I was born and to say the least, I will always wonder what he was like. I have a picture of him and I noticed our hands were alike. My grandmother Annie Bell Hawkins told me I walked like Grandfather Phillip. My mother had four siblings; thus she took a job to help her mother Annie Bell make ends meet. Neither of my grandparents on either side of our family graduated from high school.

On the other hand, my father stopped attending school in the fourth grade and never went back. My father's mother's name was Ida Mae Vann and his father's name was Samuel Vann. I remember Grandfather Sam, he was a nice man and I will always hold fond memories of him during my growing-up years. My father had five siblings, and as soon as he was old enough to work, he did.

You must understand during the 1930s that public school systems were segregated and societal pressures were very volatile for young Negro children. Just how tough were those times? My grandmother told me if a Negro walked downtown, chances are a Caucasian person would spit on them just for walking on the same side of the street. People were oftentimes cruel during that period in our history, especially in the segregated South.

The fact that neither of my parents graduated from high school resulted in a legacy in my family of people not receiving their high school diplomas. It must be understood that academic and life education are crucial to overcoming poverty. Over time, the nine Vann children would change the face of poverty through educational achievement.

My parents came from very humble beginnings and worked

hard their entire lives. They understood what it took to raise their family the right way. My mother and father worked hard to ensure all nine of their children received a good public school education. My parents were married for forty-two years before my mother went home to be with the Lord. Both of my parents worked for J.P. Taylor's Tobacco Company, which purchased, processed, and sold tobacco.

My mother analyzed and tested tobacco for J.P. Taylor's for twenty-eight years and my father drove a truck, hauling tobacco for twenty-seven years. My parents departed for work and returned home together each and every work day. Racism and prejudice was a routine part of my parents' environment and they learned how to cope with the harsh treatment they received. Opportunities were limited for Martha and Cecil; in other words, had they not been hired by J.P. Taylor's, the likelihood is they would have had to take whatever job they could find because it might be their last job for a while. My parents were luckier than most because they managed to hold onto their jobs, even though the working conditions (chemicals from the tobacco) took a toll on their health in the latter years of their lives. I asked my parents, "Mom and dad, do you think working in tobacco is causing you to have health problems?" They said, "probably son, probably."

When I reflect on poverty, it's a harsh reminder for me to always continue to set big goals for myself. My motivation to be successful stems from the very fact that I stared poverty in the face when I was a child, and it does have a face. The face of poverty looks like a starving child, a penniless man with no opportunity, and a life without hope.

Make no mistake about it—when I was young it didn't seem like we were poor because our neighbors, friends, and people in surrounding communities were in the same predicament.

❧

One day I rode with my father across town, which in southern terms means the other side of the tracks. On this fantastic voyage, my father drove through West Henderson near the country club and the homes looked like mansions. In fact, today some of them are valued over a million dollars.

One could say I had a lot of questions for my parents when my dad and I returned home. My question to my mom and dad was, "why don't we have a house like the people in West Henderson?" My parents looked at each other and said, "We don't make enough money to afford a house over there."

Thus began my quest for a better quality of life and I knew I would have to work hard to create a better standard of living for myself in the future. How poor was my family? While living in our house on 340 Skenes Avenue in Henderson, North Carolina, we didn't have indoor plumbing for quite a few years. Shocked and amazed are you? Our family had a water pump that had to be primed every day for fresh well water to drink. My parents couldn't afford hot and cold running water, which meant we had to heat our bath water on the top of the coal-burning stove or oil heater.

We were so poor we invented new words such as "roop" which is the word poor spelled backwards. I want everyone to understand from the very beginning of my life's journey that God gave my family and me the vision to look beyond our current circumstances and He showed us how to overcome a lack of financial resources and the setbacks that come with low income earning.

I will tell you something else, for a number of years we didn't have a bathroom inside our house either. We had an outhouse. In other words, whenever we had to use the potty we would venture outside to the small wooden structure or shack to relieve ourselves. Weather conditions in the spring, summer, winter, and fall are not a factor when you have to go to the toilet.

We weren't alone in this regard by any stretch of the imagination; my grandparents had outhouses, so it was not an unusual part of our existence. The only time it was unusual was when we rode by West Henderson, the side of town where the doctors, lawyers, and business owners lived. None of them had outhouses.

Our family didn't have central heating and air conditioning in the house either; during one of those hot and humid summer days in North Carolina one could lose weight simply by breathing because it really got hot. If we would have had air conditioning, we would not have known how to act. To stay cool we used floor fans. After my parents earned enough money, they purchased window fans, which were supposed to take the hot air out of the house while recycling cool air. It didn't quite work that way. In the winter time we used an oil stove and a coal burning stove, which meant I had to keep the stove full of coal; otherwise we would get up in the morning and freeze.

The lot our house was located on at 340 Skenes Avenue was sufficient for my parents' house and large enough to plant a garden. Guess who helped my father plant the garden and pick the vegetables? Lucky guess—it was me. We had corn, squash, tomatoes, butter beans, and snap peas. The insects in North Carolina would drive you crazy because they were relentless, especially during the time we were picking the vegetables from the garden.

My father planted apple trees, grapevines, and peach trees, and we were surrounded by plum trees on our property. My mother and grandmother canned the vegetables for meals in the winter time. Our garden wasn't a luxury; it was a necessity, because it was less expensive than purchasing food at a store, which was expensive back then.

My father also raised hogs, turkeys, and chickens. It was tough as a young child feeding the baby pigs, and then when they became hogs you watched them get slaughtered, cleaned in boiling water, skinned, and hung from a tree. Later in the process came the slicing and dicing, then storing the meat in a salt-filled pine box for curing. What a life, but this is what poverty demanded of our family, it was sustenance or otherwise we would have starved. Growing up in the Vann household helped me learn how to think creatively. It was important for me to learn about motivation and what it takes to be successful.

One of the funniest moments for me growing up was playing with the turkeys—real turkeys, not my friends. On one such occasion my father had to drive to town to take care of some business. I would not only feed the turkeys; I also enjoyed chasing them in the yard. One day my younger sister, Gloria Jean, was walking in the yard and didn't see the turkeys. All of a sudden one of the turkeys was staring at her. Then it went for her face and began pecking her and gobble, gobble, gobble. It was so funny I was on the ground laughing until my mother came outside to rescue my sister and then my mom tore my behind up with a switch. In the South a switch is a branch you personally have to select from a tree to get a whipping. Of course after my father returned from town, I received a repeat performance from him as well.

We also had a chicken coop, which was great because we had fresh eggs every day. In many ways my childhood was like living on a farm without actually being on one. Me and my oldest sister, Jacqueline (Jackie)—who is only a year older than me—shared as many chores as we could to lighten the load on our parents. Whenever I look in my past and need motivation, I think about how we lived back in the mid- to late 1960s. It lets me know that God can take raw talent and mold and chisel poor children and families into something greater than themselves.

Our parents believed in doing things the old-fashioned way, which included attending church every Sunday. We learned how to pray and we were taught to understand faith. I also learned about hope and determination and how it makes a difference in our lives. God allowed my family and I to see beyond our current circumstances; otherwise we would not have survived the horrific conditions we were exposed to.

The house I grew up in was a plain and basic wood structure —nothing to write home about. Our house only had three bedrooms, which meant we had to be very efficient in the use of space, especially after the twins John and Joan were born. After the twins were born, there were five children in the family.

I can remember the seminal moment in my life, which cut across the right to free speech. After Joan and John were born, my chores increased because I became my brother's keeper. I told my parents they needed to stop having children because it took up too much time from studying my schoolwork, and Jackie and I had too many chores. Cecil said, "Paul you are going to have more chores because of the statement you just made." Well, I didn't win that debate and I was given even more work to do. So much for freedom of speech.

While growing up, I wished we could afford to live in a better house. Our house was hot in the summer and cold in the winter. My parents were doing the best they could to keep a roof over our heads, and they eventually paid the entire mortgage. The house is still in our family. Make no mistake about it—I appreciate the positive example my parents set by paying off their house, considering they made very little money. Just to give you an idea of how little money my parents earned, I worked part-time for United Parcel Service (UPS) while in college and I earned more in twenty hours than my father earned in forty hours. Now you see just how little my parents earned at their jobs.

We would occasionally get a visit from a snake, and on a number of occasions snakes would make their presence felt underneath our house. My father purchased sulfur to smoke them out, and then we would have to retrieve them from underneath the house. Sometimes possums could be seen on our property, running to the water stream nearby. If my grandmother caught one of the possums, they would end up cooked in a pot.

Growing up in the segregated South helped me understand people. Many of us living in the South shared the same reality, which was poverty. Poverty doesn't care if you are a Negro or Caucasian or any other race. Poverty doesn't discriminate; people discriminate. Being the first son in a family of nine children meant I would be the first child to be tested by an unforgiving system of racism. I was not allowed to leave our yard because racial tensions were very high in the early 1960s. In fact, on the evening President Kennedy was assassinated, people set buildings on fire and it traumatized me.

My parents instilled pride and self-esteem in my sister Jackie and me. We were the only two children for roughly four years. We were taught early on not to go wandering in the wrong neighborhood or hang out with the wrong crowd; the wrong crowd was children that didn't listen to their parents. Times have really changed, haven't they? We used to pledge allegiance to the U.S. flag everyday after hoisting it up the pole at school. My, my, my, times have really changed.

The foundation for the Vann family was the church. My mother's side of the family attended Shiloh Baptist Church of Henderson, North Carolina, and we have been members of Shiloh for over 120 years. My siblings and I were baptized in the church. We attended and worked there for as long as we can remember.

The church is the Vann's rock and foundation, just as God is the creator of the world and is all power. In the formative years we learned about Jesus the Saviour of the world at Shiloh Baptist Church. I learned of God's power and second chances in life, revival, and most importantly the resurrection.

The one thing that kept me going was the first time I heard

about Jesus Christ being crucified, dying for our sins—and then on the third day he arose from the grave and ascended into the heavens. It gave me hope, and in life hope and faith can take us wherever we want to go.

My father's side of the family attended Red Bud Baptist Church in Henderson, North Carolina. My grandparents attended Red Bud practically their entire lives. We believed in God, and that is the foundation for our family. Martha and Cecil's son Paul's fondest memory is attending Sunday church services and programs and he credits his Christian upbringing for his success.

Growing up at Shiloh Baptist Church and adhering to the teachings of the Bible allowed me to understand the way I should live and to understand all things were possible through Jesus Christ. America is strong because she allows for freedom of worship.

The first school I ever attended was L.B.Yancey Elementary, which was a three-minute walk from our house on Skenes Avenue. I could run to Yancey in a couple of minutes. All of my teachers were African-American until the fifth grade, when integration and busing began. In the sixth grade, my sister and I were bussed from South Henderson to Pinkston Street Middle School, which was located quite a distance from our community.

A year later my older sister Jackie and I were bussed and attended seventh through ninth grades at Henderson Junior High, which was located near downtown Henderson. There were more positives than negatives attending an all black school because the layer of understanding between like-minded people worked better prior to the signing of important civil rights laws. The Civil Rights Act was introduced by President Dwight Eisenhower in 1957, a year before I was born. President Kennedy introduced the civil rights bill in 1963; sadly, he didn't live to see it come into law.

I began elementary school in September, 1964—a couple of

months after the Civil Rights Act was signed on July 2. Were it not for the passage of the 1964 Civil Rights Act, I might not have written this book.

Once our school system became integrated, it took time for relationships between African-American parents and Caucasian teachers to take root and manifest itself from a trust perspective. It's important to remember that minorities with limited opportunities distrusted people in the majority (Caucasians) because they were perceived to be a part of the obstacles and hurdles leading to unequal rights and lack of opportunity.

Integration of public schools in North Carolina also resulted in a large number of highly qualified African-American teachers and school administrators unjustifiably losing their jobs to Caucasians. This caused a lot of friction in Henderson. While attending elementary school, all of my teachers were African-Americans. They contacted my parents to schedule meetings in our house. My teachers visited our home to discuss how I was doing academically and how I behaved in class.

You talk about pressure! I would be sitting beside my mother thinking I had home court advantage, only to discover my parents and teachers had the same goal in mind: molding me into the man I would someday become. It's very important to listen to our parents and respect them and our teachers because they truly care about us achieving academic success.

Shortly after one of my teachers left our house, the likelihood is that I was disciplined because of how I was acting in school. You don't see a lot of this happening in school anymore, and if I could make a recommendation, even though my parents didn't graduate from high school they played an intricate role in me succeeding in school because they were actively involved in the process.

Martha and Cecil Vann knew all of my teachers, principals, and even the substitute teachers. In retrospect, the teachers and principals were our extended family. My parents wanted all nine of their children to succeed academically because they wanted us to have a better quality of life than they had.

While in middle school I always knew I would leave my hometown to see the world and make something out of myself. Perhaps it was divine intervention or it was simply my destiny. The single act that solidified my insight was a trip to New York City to visit my relatives that migrated from Henderson, North Carolina. Some of my relatives lived in Harlem and others in Mount Vernon, New York. First of all, we had to convince my father to let me visit my relatives. Once he agreed, I knew the trip to New York would change my life forever.

Other than visiting Raleigh or Durham, North Carolina, I had never visited a large city prior to traveling to New York. After riding an hour and twenty minutes on I-85 north approaching Richmond, Virginia, I saw tall buildings. Henderson, North Carolina still doesn't have any tall buildings. I was having an eye-opening experience, to say the least.

After arriving in New York City, it dawned on me that I had never seen so many people at one time in my entire life. I want you to know I had a crook in my neck because I was looking up at so many skyscrapers. People know whether or not you are a tourist because the locals rarely look up at the tall buildings.

I stayed with my mother's sister, my Aunt Ruth Harris, for a couple of nights, then with my mom's other sister, Carolyn Faye Hawkins Chisolm. My mother's brother, Uncle John Hawkins, who we call "Dewey" and Aunt Virginia, who we call "Gin" lived in Mount Vernon, New York. Everyone gathered at Ruth's house to visit me while staying in New York because she was an excellent cook. Ruth could cook so good she would make you slap your other aunt.

Ruth and Carolyn were my angels growing up. They taught me a lot about life and listened to me and always offered me the opportunity to live with them in New York if I decided to leave

Henderson after high school. New York City was too big for me at the time, so I took it off my list of places to live.

While visiting New York City, I had never seen so many people in my life, especially people that looked like me. They wore nice clothes, looked like business people, and walked with an air of confidence, as if they had somewhere important to go.

My Aunt Ruth took me shopping to purchase school clothes. I remember going into Macy's Department store and seeing all of the displays and saying to myself, these people must have a lot of money to be able to afford these clothes. I was overcome by seeing so many people on the train because we were packed in like sardines. When I went to sleep that night I had a nightmare that I was still on the train. The city life is aggressive compared to where I was growing up.

My trip to New York to visit my relatives provided me with the experience I needed to see how different life could be for me in the future.

After returning home, I talked to my sister Jackie about what I saw and what I did while in New York. She said, "You are talking proper," which means my Southern drawl had somewhat dissipated. After my trip to New York, I changed because I experienced a different environment compared to the one I was growing up in, and my quest to see the world was only just beginning. I came home renewed and invigorated because I could see beyond my current circumstance, which was one of poverty.

My sister Jackie was a grade ahead of me, and after successfully completing middle school, I entered Vance Senior High School in September 1973. It seemed as though time was passing by at a fast pace and in a few years I would be graduating from high school. The one thing that stuck in my mind was graduating from high school and receiving my diploma. I began to see the possibilities of achieving academic success and pursuing success of some kind.

I had to overcome the educational legacy of having parents

and grandparents who didn't receive their diplomas. I am confident that my parents were expecting my sister Jackie and I to be the first children in our family to earn our high school diplomas.

Since Jackie was the oldest child she would be the first child in the Vann family to graduate from high school. Jackie was the first born child in the Vann family but unfortunately she decided to leave school in the eleventh grade. I am proud of her for going back to school to earn her diploma. By returning to school she proved she had courage. It's important to never give up on your dreams. Jackie had the Vann spirit of never giving up on achieving your dreams.

The event that impeded my ability to study more was my parents opening a small community grocery store. I started working in the store when I was twelve years old. It was called Vann's Grocery; very original, as you can see. The small store was built around an old tree and initially we sold fish and produce. Every Thursday, the fish were delivered to our store, and I had to clean them. I didn't like eating fish when I was growing up because I had to see them every single week for what seemed like eternity.

My parents didn't make a lot of money in this business venture, but it helped me understand and appreciate the entrepreneurial skills required for business. The store was located on our property, which meant I didn't have to go far to work. Eventually, the business expanded, and we sold canned goods, sodas, cigarettes, meat, candy, and coal for cast iron stoves.

I will never forget the first time my father told me to deliver a bag of coal to one of our neighbors. I lifted the bag onto my shoulder and walked to their house. By the time I arrived, the bag had burst. Coal was all over their porch and I was covered with residue.

Don't get me wrong—I enjoyed working in my parents' store. The most memorable day consisted of me arriving home from school and going to work. The bread delivery driver arrived at his regular scheduled time. The bread delivery man asked me, "How are you doing today Paul?" I said, "I'm doing great today, how about you? Now that we have stacked the bread, let me get the money to pay you," I said. Step, step, step, I'm in front of the cash register about to press the cash register key. I really believe our brains are faster than computers, because my brain told my hands, "don't touch the cash register key because you will feel pain." By this time my brain sent another message to my feet and I immediately ran past the bread delivery man out of our store. The delivery man followed me out of the store and asked me, "Is everything alright, what's wrong?" After catching my breath, I said, "A snake is on the cash register and you won't be receiving payment for the bread today because I'm not going back in the store today." A black snake was crawling on the cash register keys and I freaked out because I almost touched it. As far as I was concerned, the bread company was not going to be paid that day. After closing the store, I had no plans of going back in because the snake almost bit me. After arriving home from work, my father said, "Go back in the store and why did you close it in the first place?" I said, "Snakes and I don't get along and I'm not going back in the store this evening."

In many ways, I missed out on a lot of my childhood because I had to work in our store after school and on the weekends. When I reflect on my childhood, I must say that working in our store helped me learn how to sell and work with people because of the interaction with the customers. Dating was limited for me because I was working most of the time, and I couldn't leave the store.

Fortunately, I had the guidance of my relatives to help me understand and appreciate the options available to me. Aunt Carolyn Faye sat down with me to discuss what I planned to do after earning my high school diploma. Carolyn Faye said, "Paul, what do you want to do after you graduate from high school? Do you want to work at a factory, join the military, or attend college?" It was an easy choice: the word "college" didn't rhyme with the word "work," so it was a logical choice for me. Just kidding.

I was presented with an opportunity to make some educational gains for our family and I was up for the challenge. In my neighborhood, I was always considered to be smart academically. But I considered myself to be an average student in school. I knew I could have done better if I had better study habits. Working in the store didn't help. Two pivotal events occurred in my life that changed me forever, and I will share them with you.

The first event was my goal to play football in the eleventh grade. I wanted to try out for the high school football team; however, I was competing against high school athletes that started playing football in middle school—or in some cases, the pee wee league. I had a lot of catching up to do in a short amount of time. Prior to making the leap athletically, I had to ask my parents if I could try out for the team. My mother said yes, but my father said no because he wanted me to work in Vann's Grocery store.

My Grandmother Ida Mae Vann was getting up in years and was living by herself, after talking with her she talked to my father about me living with her. Living with my grandmother provided me the opportunity to play high school football. After all, I only had a couple of years to finish high school before graduating. Talk about motivation! My Grandmother Ida Mae Vann welcomed me into her home with open arms. Grandma Ida said, "Cecil, having Paul around will help me manage my house better; besides I'm getting up in age, you know."

"Yes ma'am," my father sarcastically said. My grandmother supported my decision to play football because she knew it would make me happy and besides she was living in a big house all by herself and could use some help with the chores. It helped me understand relationships because I learned how to balance my family life with my academic life. Playing football was important to me because it gave me the opportunity to learn teamwork, discipline, and resilience. The things I learned participating in team sports led to greater leadership opportunities for me in the future.

I was motivated to risk everything for what I believed in, but more than anything, I knew I had to become good at playing the game of football. I worked hard to be a good football player, and played on the junior varsity team at Vance Senior High. Our team did not win a lot of football games; however, I obtained invaluable experience to prepare me for my senior year.

Over the course of the summer, I worked hard in the gym, lifting weights every single day, making my body stronger so I could compete with the more experienced football players during my senior year. I took whatever job I could to make money to help make ends meet. I woke up at 5:00 a.m. and waited for a tobacco farmer to arrive in his truck with other workers. We primed tobacco, which involves picking tobacco leaves off tobacco stalks on acre after acre of farmland. We typically finished working at noon and—make no mistake about it—priming tobacco is hard work, and dangerous as well.

Priming tobacco is a tough job because the working conditions are dangerous. One has to be aware of snakes, spiders, bugs, chemicals on the tobacco leaf, mud, avoiding getting run over by a tractor, and heat stroke.

Priming tobacco was one of the hardest jobs I have ever held in my life. This reminds me of the time when I worked for a tobacco farmer. One day, after finishing up for the day, he dropped me off at my house. I was expecting to receive thirty dollars, but instead he paid me one dollar. This kind of thing happens to people in poverty every single day; it just happened to be my turn. My father had to restrain me because I was not going to be misused by someone who owed me money. Cooler heads prevailed and I understood the lesson my father was teaching me, the reality that life isn't always fair.

My dad looked at me and said, "I told you not to work for him," which didn't help matters. But I learned a valuable lesson that day, and it was to seal the deal before all is said and done. In other words, in life you get what you negotiate. In other words, I should have received thirty dollars that day but I didn't. Now I know how to seal the deal because that tobacco farmer made me a keen businessman.

My father knew a lot of people and he drove me to their houses to mow their lawns. I will never forget the times he dropped me off to mow lawns for people. They paid me two dollars to mow the lawn. Gas was about thirty-five cents a gallon, so I made a profit. The goal for me was to mow the lawn as fast as I could, because the sun would wear me down.

My parents did a great job raising my siblings and me, and I give them credit for reining me in when they had to. I could have gotten into trouble, achieving nothing in life. People sometimes complain about the family they grew up in. When I reflect on my upbringing, no other parents could have done as great a job with us nine children.

At the beginning of my senior year, I had become a chiseled athlete because I had worked out in the gym all summer. I changed my physical body, which increased my confidence, foot speed, and endurance. I changed so much that most of my teammates didn't recognize me.

After starting at defensive end on the junior varsity team, I was determined to make the first team during my senior year of high school, and I did. During football practice I was able to do anything I set my mind to do. I was stronger, quicker, and faster than almost everyone on the football team, except our running back, who went on to the National Football League. I motivated myself to excel at the highest level of football for my high school team, and to be a part of one of the best teams in the state of North Carolina.

In August 1975, after weeks of hot and humid practice, Coach Tony Oates named the starting offensive and defensive teams. I was named starting right defensive end for the Vance Senior High Vikings and proved to myself that I could do the impossible—to make the starting team with only one year of experience. In other words, I set a lofty goal and reached it, just as I had planned it. Let this be a lesson for everyone, if you want something bad enough and put in the work to earn it, you can achieve any goal you set.

It should be no surprise to anyone that I was going to make it because I had everything going for me. First of all, my father was totally against me playing football. My mother and grandmother supported me because they knew how much it meant to me. I instantly became very popular at school because I was on the starting defense team.

As life has a way of balancing things out, oftentimes I would be playing defensive end, the play would come to my side of the field, and I would take on three or sometimes four blockers and still be able to tackle the running back or quarterback.

Over the loudspeaker, one could hear the radio announcer say, "Fantastic defensive play made by #64 Paul Vann." My entire family would either be attending or listening to the game on the radio. After the game, my father was so proud of me that he wanted to talk about the game. All of our neighbors would be talking about the game to my father and he was full of himself because his son was doing so well.

Even though my father didn't think I should play high school football, in the end he was my number one fan. I was able to find balance as a student/athlete in high school, and it made me a better person for going against all odds. I was motivated to excel academically, and from a whole-person perspective.

The Vance Senior High School Vikings won their first five

games of the year, lost to our crosstown rivals, Oxford Webb, and ended the season with seven wins and three losses. The Vikings went to the state playoffs, but lost the first game because the center hiked the ball over the punter's head, resulting in a turnover that led to our opponent scoring and winning the game. This ended our football season; however, the life lessons I took from playing football would remain with me for the rest of my life.

Now that football season was over, I needed to buckle down with my schoolwork and grades. The second event that had a great impact on me and was pivotal was a meeting with my guidance counselor. I scheduled the meeting with Ms. Waddell to discuss my high school academic performance leading up to graduation, and my consideration for attending college.

I went to Ms. Waddell's office and she stated, "Paul, you are doing just fine in school and if you keep your grades up you will graduate on time." Then she went on to say, "Paul, I don't believe you have what it takes to be a successful college student, and there is no need to discuss your prospects for attending college because you don't have what it takes." I was sitting directly in front of Ms. Waddell's desk and if her desk wasn't in front of me I believe I would have fallen out of my chair in disbelief.

My guidance counselor was sitting in front of me telling me I couldn't achieve a goal. I was not about to have my dream deferred because of someone's opinion. I would have nothing to do with her opinion. I left the meeting and headed back to class.

I was fit to be tied, hurt, and disappointed to hear what my guidance counselor had to say. After leaving school that day I went to my parent's house to talk with them about my meeting with Ms. Waddell. First my mother told me, "Paul, forget about what Ms. Waddell said at your meeting today." Then my father said, "Son, come up with a plan and strategy to successfully graduate from high school and start applying to various colleges."

My success plan for improving my grades in high school involved both time management and goal setting. I took all of my free time before, during, and after school including the weekend to read, review, and study every single class I needed to successfully graduate. It came down to properly managing my time and studying without ceasing, I became a proverbial bookworm and it made all the difference in me being accepted into college.

The reason why it's important for children to listen to their parents is because our parents have dealt with various degrees of adversity, hurdles, and obstacles in life and our parents know how to overcome setbacks. In my particular case, the good news I received from Ms. Waddell is that I was going to graduate from high school, which meant I was going to be the first individual in my family to do so.

I confronted another obstacle leading up to graduating from high school. It occurred just after the football season ended. My oldest sister Jackie was dating a young man that contracted hepatitis; it was communicable. My mother, sister, and I visited my sister's boyfriend in the hospital. It was a visit we probably should have avoided.

Less than two weeks later, I became very ill and my eyes took on a yellowish tint. My mother took me to the hospital, and as luck would have it I had hepatitis as well. I entered Maria Parham Hospital in Henderson the week of Thanksgiving 1975. On the first day, I was given my hospital pajamas and was assigned to my room and I was bored. My mother contacted the principal and my teachers to inform them that I would be out of school until I fully recovered.

On Tuesday, the second day of my hospitalization, I was examined by my doctor and given antibiotics to help me recover. When I entered the hospital, I weighed one hundred sixty-three pounds. Over the course of a week in the hospital, I lost twenty pounds.

Late Tuesday evening I was bored and didn't have anything to read. I opened the drawer of the nightstand and the only thing in there was a version of the King James Bible. I began to read the Bible. Since I frequently attended church, it was in keeping for me to read the Bible.

As I read, the Holy Spirit began to minister unto me spiritually, so I continued to read the Bible without ceasing. The Holy Spirit revealed to me that I would be healed, and I was. Prior to catching hepatitis, I was in the process of deciding which college to apply to, and what discipline I was going to concentrate in and major in at college. Again the Holy Spirit interceded and informed me that before I was to leave for college, I needed to give my life to Christ. After leaving the hospital, I should go directly to Shiloh Baptist Church to be baptized in water and begin working in the church.

In other words, it was not a coincidence that I was in the hospital. I believe I was meant to be in the hospital at this time in my life because it allowed me an opportunity to listen to my inner voice. I want everyone to know that I didn't receive any visitors in the hospital except my doctor and my Uncle John and Aunt Virginia, who were visiting family in Henderson during the Thanksgiving holiday.

A few people from my church also visited me because they typically visited sick and shut-in members of the church. No one really knew I was in the hospital except my family, the principal, and my teachers. My hospitalization represented an important call on my life from God and this single event changed my life forever.

During the week of Thanksgiving, 1975, I gave my life to God through Jesus Christ and I was never the same again. All I know is that I wanted to live a life pleasing to God. I knew I would do some amazing things in life because my hospital experience prepared me for the impossible. I was recovering quite well. My doctor said, "Paul, I will be releasing you from the hospital on

Saturday." I wanted to go home and begin my spiritual journey.

My nurse asked me, "Paul, would you like a wheelchair?" I laughed and said, "No way, I'm fine and won't need a wheelchair; besides I've rested enough and can walk on my own power." My father arrived to pick me up, so I said I was fine and didn't need a wheelchair. After I stood up and walked a few steps, I almost collapsed. I asked the nurse, "Can I have one of those wheelchairs, please?"

My mother had a beautiful smile on her face and was glad to see me. My dad stopped by our house so everyone could see how much weight I had lost; my siblings could not believe how different I looked. Then my dad took me to his mother's house to stay. A week later I went straight to my pastor and requested to be baptized in water. I took on duties in church and everyone was amazed at my transformation—I didn't look or act the same after my hospitalization.

While hospitalized, the Holy Spirit told me I would be attending Shaw University in Raleigh, North Carolina, and that I would be a business major in college. I would be playing football or participating on the track and field team. All of these things were coming to me in my mind and I wrote them down on paper. The one thing I did not have at the time was money for tuition and fees to attend college. So I began to pray for the answers and I listened to the voices on the inside that were directing my life like no other time I could remember.

After returning to school, my classmates and teachers were amazed at how much weight I had lost and how much better I looked. Everyone could see the change in me and they were glad to see me. I was very popular in school because of the exposure from playing football. I began to fill out applications to college and knew Shaw University would be the college I would be attending. I planned on playing football; however, I still had to contend with obtaining money to cover tuition, room and board.

In order to help my financial situation, I decided to participate on the track team to help obtain an athletic scholarship, and discovered that I was a gifted runner. I had never participated on the track team before my senior year, and didn't know what to expect. I kept on learning and making a contribution as I focused my energies on making the football team at Shaw University.

Track practice began in the spring of 1976—five months before graduation. I didn't even know what events I would be selected to run because I did not have experience in track and field. I loved running and enjoyed the practices, which were grueling; we began each practice session with a one-mile run before sprinting, calisthenics, and endurance work. Then the team began sustained sprint work and we all learned how to run like track and field athletes. I discovered how to train my body to do whatever I asked of it.

Our high school track team needed an 800-yard dash runner, a 400-yard dash runner, and a mile relay runner. Guess which three events I ran? I had never run in a track meet my entire life, but that's not the half of it! Our school did not have a track to practice on either. The Vance Senior High track team practiced on its football practice field. I never knew exactly what to expect while running the curves, or start and finish of a race, but through vision and sheer determination I learned.

Not having a practice field worked to our advantage because we were so eager to get on a real track to show what we had. It was a disadvantage because we never had a home field (track) advantage because we always ran on our opponent's track.

Running track helped me learn discipline and to stand alone if need be, which meant I learned how to cope with doing things on my own. Track and field is a team sport, which means you still have people counting on you for points for your specific events. Running the 800-yard dash was a test of speed and endurance. In order to be good at it you must practice, practice, practice. Being a novice at the 800-yard dash only meant I had to work harder than my competitors, and I put in the hard work, resulting in me winning my first five races.

I will never forget my first race because I did not know what to expect. In fact, the only thing I kept in mind was to run around the track as fast as I could and win the race. I won the race because I didn't know what I didn't know, which meant I simply did what I was told to do by my coach. That was to give my all in the race. If I did this, I would win, and I did.

I won my first 800-yard dash competition in a time of two minutes and five seconds (2:05) which meant on average I could run a quarter of a mile in one minute and two seconds. Not bad for a novice. What motivational lesson did I take from running track and field? I discovered who I was as an individual and as a teammate. I did not want to let my coach, team, or myself down, and that was motivation enough for me to win most of my competitions.

I also ran the quarter-mile and I had a teammate named Nathan. He was very good and we put on some classic sprint races in practice and on the track in order to produce a fast mile relay team. Since I ran the 800-yard dash and the 400, I was the logical choice for the anchor leg of the mile relay team, because I had sufficient time to rest between events. Typically, if an opposing team had a twenty-yard lead on us going into the last lap, I could catch and pass them for the win. We did this on numerous occasions.

The only person I lost to in the 800-yard dash was a runner that eventually won the state title. So again I say to everyone, even though I only ran track in order to improve my speed for football, I had the gift for running in me my entire life. I accomplished my goal of improving my speed and I learned through God we all have greatness on the inside of us. All we have to do is discover the talents and abilities we are given at birth.

The biggest mistake I ever made in track and field was not participating in the Amateur Athletic Union (AAU) Junior Olympic competitions. The reason why I didn't attend a scheduled meet is because I was out late the night before at a party. Poor choices can yield poor results, and if I had to do it all over again, I would have gotten the rest I needed to compete against the best.

By this time my dad was on board with anything I wanted to do because he was very proud of my accomplishments. The Vann name was in the public because I played football—this is common in small towns. I lettered in football and track and field, and was on my way to being the first child in a family of nine children to graduate from high school.

Being first in anything means a lot of people helped you along the way. First of all, I have to give praise to God because He allowed me the time to listen to my inner voice while hospitalized; little did I know that single event would be the catalyst for the rest of my life, even today. I am a believer, and if I did not have anything monetarily, my faith and belief in God would sustain me.

My parents played the most important role in my success because they encouraged me to do my best in school. Martha and Cecil knew I had to be the one to break the legacy of family members not receiving their high school diplomas, and I did what I needed to do to break the cycle of poverty through educational achievement.

I also have to thank all of my teachers, who believed in me, and my football and track and field coaches—they taught me so many valuable lessons about determination, sacrifice, and resilience. I give many thanks to my classmates, who did their very best by being themselves and being good friends to me and my teammates in sports. We were the chosen ones and being a Vance High Viking is an honor never to be forgotten.

Graduation time was drawing nearer and I had forgotten the conversation I had with Ms. Waddell because it was simply one person's opinion versus the reality unfolding for me academically. I graduated from high school on June 9, 1976. It was a big deal for me to graduate, and my relatives from New York attended the graduation ceremony. Family members from out of town who attended were Aunt Ruth Hawkins and Carolyn Hawkins Chisolm from New York City, my mother, and a few of my siblings.

The high school graduation ceremony was held at the Henderson Junior High football stadium. My finest hour had arrived and now it was time for me to accept my diploma. The announcer stated the following words: "accepting his diploma is Paul Lawrence Vann." I walked up, received my diploma from the principal, shook his hand, and turned my tassel. I broke the educational legacy of a family who for so long had done without academic opportunity, and began a new legacy, which resulted in all eight of my siblings receiving their high school diplomas. Half of us received a bachelor's degree and/or master's degree.

After the ceremony I ran into the crowd, kissed my mother, and told her the diploma was for her and my dad and the rest of our family. When I graduated, they graduated with me. I didn't graduate alone because I had the support and love of my family and they all wanted me to do well. I did it against all odds. Some of my classmates didn't make it because of unfortunate incidents such as a car accident before graduation, or they dropped out of school.

I received over three hundred dollars from friends and family members at graduation, and was hired for a summer job working at the Henderson Recreation Department to earn money for college. After applying for grants, I received a Pell Grant to pay for college the first year of school. My parents didn't have money for college because they had eight other children to feed and clothe.

"Paul, you are a blessing to our family," said Martha Vann, my mother. I knew what my mother was saying, and I will never forget it, because she knew there was much more in store for me than a high school diploma and she was right.

More importantly, my mother knew if one of her children graduated from high school the rest would follow, and again she was right. Being a blessing to my parents and family was an honor, and I would not disappoint them or myself. At the end of my high school years I knew how to motivate myself and others around me, and I also knew I was never alone because God is always with me and blesses me.

Henderson, North Carolina, is my hometown where I was born and raised. I want all of the citizens living in Henderson to understand we have all come a long way on our journey together. If it were not for my family, community, and hometown, I would not be the person I am today. I salute you all and thank you for preparing me for life.

ACTION PLAN #1

Seeing Beyond Our Current Circumstances

NEITHER MY PARENTS NOR GRANDPARENTS GRADUATED FROM high school; however, it did not stop them from encouraging my siblings and me to earn our high school diplomas. We all have different legacies of one kind or another; however, one of the most important decisions we should make is to see beyond our current circumstances. Most importantly, we need faith and belief in ourselves in order to avoid the pitfalls and hurdles in life so we can achieve our goals and live our life with purpose. I didn't have an example to follow in terms of earning my diploma, bachelor's degree, or master's degree, but I believed in God and trusted Him to help me see beyond my lack of money, opportunity, and resources.

Please take some time to think about the barriers standing between you and your success. Write down seven things you want to overcome and achieve. You will realize you have the power to see beyond your current circumstances, be it mission-oriented, or personal.

1. _____

2. _____

3. _____

4. _____

5. _____

6. _____

7. _____

Retain your list and refer to it often, because it represents your new flight plan and marching orders. You will have the ability to see yourself achieving each and every goal you set because you are a winner.

My parents instilled high self-esteem in my siblings and me, which helped us conquer the poor educational legacy in our family. Likewise, you will need a high level of self-esteem to propel you to overcome obstacles in your daily life. Oftentimes in life the difference between success and failure is having the courage and belief to see our plans through to fruition. Don't give up or give in. Up, up, and away!

ACTION PLAN #2

Setting Our Table for Success

NOW THAT WE CAN SEE BEYOND OUR CURRENT CIRCUMSTANCES, it's time for us to set the table for our success. Just as we sit down at a table in a restaurant, we have a place setting that consists of a napkin, spoon, fork, and knife. We also need a place setting in order to achieve success. Successful people never achieve success by osmosis. For example, the power of positive thinking, which is the starting point for achieving success, is great; however, unless we invoke the power of positive doing (action step), we will fall short of our desired goals.

Please list the top five goals you envision yourself achieving in order to set your table for success in the military with your organization, unit, squadron, battalion, and/or with your military family member(s).

1. _____

2. _____

3. _____

4. _____

5. _____

What is your passion?

Of the five goals you listed, which one keeps you up at night? In other words, if you were selected to take command of your company, unit, squadron, or force, and it's the exact slot you were dreaming of, would you do it for free? Which goal will not allow you to sleep because you are so excited about achieving it? You will discover your passion through your desire to complete your place setting at your table of success. Of the five goals, which has the highest rank on your list?

My passion is_____.

In elementary school, my fifth grade teacher asked me what I wanted to be when I grew up. I said an astronaut. Even though I didn't know what I would be when I grew up, I dreamed big. After college I became an Air Force leader and worked on space programs with the Air National Guard. In many respects, I lived part of my initial dream by working on space programs. It's never too late to make a command decision to live your dreams. What is your dream? _____

_____

_____

_____

"Believe in your dreams and they will lead you to your destiny."
—Paul Lawrence Vann

～ 2 ～

You Have to Know Who You Are

*As a being of power, intelligence, and love and the Lord of his
own thoughts, man holds the key to every situation, and contains
within himself that transforming and regenerative agency by
which he may make himself what he wills.*

—James Allen

THE SUMMER OF 1976 WAS AS HOT AND HUMID AS ANY ON record.
I was hired by the Henderson Recreation Department to help
construct Fox Pond Park, a multi-purpose park equipped with
tennis courts, a softball field for children, fishing and camp-
ing sites, and an outdoor amphitheater. Through determination and long hours of work, my cousin Eddie Hicks, Shelton
McKnight, and I put our muscle power on the line. We physi-
cally laid the foundation for the park by securing and laying
gravel, lining telegraph poles for parking lots, and clearing
walking paths for nature walks.

Eddie was one of my first role models. He attended East
Carolina University on a football scholarship, and was a star
running back doing great things on the football team at the
national level. He was a tremendous athlete and a very good
person who had the determination to be successful. Eddie
played for coach Pat Dye during the period that the East
Carolina Pirate football team was gaining prominence in the
late 1970s and early 1980s. Eddie was gifted, and as fast as any
man in the world. Shelton and I learned a lot about football
and ourselves by talking and being around Eddie.

It was realistic to believe I could be as good an athlete as Eddie. Deep down inside, I was more focused on tackling my books because I was confident I could do it through educational achievement during my college years. I admired Eddie because he worked hard at being a good football player, and he went on to play for the New York Giants, Philadelphia Eagles, and the Winnipeg Blue Bombers in the Canadian Football League.

Shelton and I, along with three other Vance Senior High School graduates, applied to and were accepted at Shaw University, a small Historically Black College and University (HBCU) located in Raleigh, North Carolina. Shaw University was founded in 1865 and is the oldest HBCU in the South. It's located forty-five miles south of Henderson. I used the money I earned from working at the recreation department for my expenses at Shaw University when I entered in August 1976. The rest of my expenses were covered by the Pell Grant, along with money I earned working part-time as an electrician apprentice with one of our family friends—an electrical contractor in Raleigh.

I decided against playing football at Shaw University because I had a lot to prove academically. Besides, Shaw University was going to terminate its football program a year or two later. I am happy to say Shaw University reconstituted its football program in 2002, and compiled winning records for two consecutive years. In 2004, Shaw won the Central Intercollegiate Athletic Association (CIAA) Championship. On December 4th Shaw also won Pioneer Bowl VII, defeating Tuskegee Institute in an exciting come-from-behind victory culminating in a 30–28 victory and ending the season 10–2. Way to go, Shaw Bears!

At Shaw University I focused primarily on my academics. Since I had overcome the legacy of family members not graduating from high school, I knew I had to make my time in college count. I had eight siblings watching me wade into the academic waters of college, and I wanted them to follow my lead and know that it was safe to follow me.

The values I learned from my parents and other family members played a pivotal role in my academic success in college. During my freshman year of college, I hit the books really hard, ensuring the things I could control were in check. In other words, I could control the grades I received simply by studying into the early hours of the morning. I wasn't satisfied with merely passing— I needed to keep a high grade point average throughout my college years.

My mother and father, grandmothers, and aunts and uncles taught me a lot about being myself. They knew the secret to success rests in one being one's self no matter how much success one achieves in life. Success in life means someone else helped us attain our goals and high achievement.

The most profound thing people can choose to understand is one thing and one thing only: "you have to know who you are as a person." In other words, until you know who you are you may change with any wind of doctrine. The lesson passed down from my mother and father is that no matter what circumstance you find yourself in, you will thrive in it as long as you are yourself and know the decision you made is the right one in the eyes of God.

My college experience was wonderful because it gave me an opportunity to know who I was as a person. I contemplated majoring in engineering when I enrolled at Shaw University; however, after looking at the course requirements, I decided to major in business management with a minor in accounting. All of the years I worked in our family grocery store prepared me for a business degree.

My grades at the end of the first semester were good, but not great—there was room for improvement. The improvement would come in the form of discipline, which meant I would take all of my spare time, go to the library and study until it closed or until I understood everything my subjects required.

❦

Carolyn Faye Hawkins Chisolm was my mother's sister. I absolutely adored her because she was such a beautiful lady inside and out. Carolyn was not only my aunt, but my best friend as well, and if I have any talent in writing and speaking it truly came from being around Carolyn. She was an advocate for civil rights and was very outspoken on the injustices that occurred in our society. She stood up for her rights no matter where she was.

The low point of my freshman year came from a phone call I received from my cousin Sandra Lee Wilson. I was in my room studying when one of my dorm mates told me to come to the phone, I hurried to the phone. My cousin Sandra Lee informed me that Aunt Carolyn had been murdered in New York City. The police report stated that Carolyn's husband's cousin broke into their apartment and killed her.

When the police arrived, they found my aunt in a pool of blood. Fortunately, he didn't kill her two-year-old daughter, who was found in the blood of her mother. As much as I had prayed that God would keep me in my right mind, I wanted the murderer put away for life, but he wasn't.

Losing Carolyn was like losing a part of my being because I have never met anyone with such a beautiful heart and intellect as my dear aunt. Carolyn by far was one of the most influential people in my life, and I will carry her memory with me for the rest of my days.

I believe the spiritual experience that occurred in Maria Parham Hospital prepared me for the horrific event that took my aunt's life. Carolyn was a tremendous writer and had a number of her poems printed in newspapers in New York City. She also was present with me the night I discovered one of my gifts, the gift of dreams.

My parents had asked Carolyn to watch after my sister Jackie and me because they were scheduled to attend the annual Christmas Party hosted by J.P. Taylor's and the American Federation of Labor-Congress of Industrial Organizations (AFL-CIO).

It was cold that day with minimal prospects for snow. Jackie was twelve years old, and I was ten.

After Carolyn arrived at our house to stay for the evening, my parents departed for the Christmas party. I was feeling really tired and fell fast asleep. As I recall, I had a nightmare and a couple of hours later I awakened to discover that my aunt was concerned because I had sweated so profusely while asleep. Carolyn asked me what I was dreaming about and I told her I dreamt that my parents were in a car accident and that I could see it as if I was there when it happened. She reassured me that everything was going to be all right, and as we were talking, eventually it began to snow.

As midnight approached, we became more concerned because my parents had not arrived home from the Christmas party. An hour later, a member of the Vance County Sheriff's Department drove his car into our driveway and my parents got out of his car. My parents had been in a car accident because of the heavy snowfall and had sustained minor injuries. My aunt looked at me and then began to cry because she knew I had mentioned the car accident to her earlier that evening and she told my parents about it.

Throughout my life I have dreamt of events that eventually happened in my life. Some of the dreams take years to occur; others occur within days. I believe I have the gift of dreams, and even though I can't remember all of them, when I find myself living out the dream, I simply thank God for being God and giving me the gift of being a dreamer.

The most consistent dream I have is that of flying, and as you will discover later in this book, I joined the United States Air Force, which proved to me that dreams really do come true.

You have to know who you are in life because we are all going to be challenged to make tough decisions, and a testament to who we are is the quality of our decisions. By knowing who we are we can live with the consequences of our decisions.

You have to know who you are in order to trust God and yourself. For example, I was willing to work as an electrician apprentice without having the experience or skill to work in such a dangerous field. I prayed a lot about the work I performed. I knew it would help me pay for my tuition and fees in college; furthermore, I trusted my employer, who on occasion would let me stick my hand in a panel box and get shocked in order to teach me the particulars about the profession. It was electrifying to say the least, and it was a win-win situation for my employer and I because he received the needed labor and I received the money I needed for college.

After Christmas break of 1976, I went to Henderson for the holidays and helped out around the house and in our community grocery store. I talked to my parents and siblings about college life. I was very emphatic about letting everyone know I would not be coming back to our hometown to work after graduation because of the lack of employment opportunities.

I was simply changing. When one attends college, one grows academically and intellectually. As young adults, our minds never go back to what it used to be. Our minds continue to expand and develop—and that's exactly what was happening to me. The meeting with my guidance counselor continued to stick with me, and I used the conversation for motivation every time I felt burned out from studying so much.

I began practicing for the track team during the Christmas break, and was on schedule for making a contribution to the track team at Shaw University. It didn't matter to me that Shaw did not have a track to practice on because numerous athletes win medals in the Olympics without their school having a track, much less a track team.

Edwin Moses competed in the 400-meter hurdles and was the track and field athlete I admired, because he was determined to be the best in track and field. Morehouse College, the school Edwin attended, didn't have a track to practice on, so as far as I was concerned, I was more than prepared.

Instead of competing in the 800-meter dash, I decided to compete in the 400-meter dash and did well. I knew I was not going to remain in track and field because my priorities had changed. My priority was to earn good grades, which meant I would have to study harder in order to participate in track practice to keep my grades up. I did just fine; I contributed to the track team, was on the relay team, and was noted for having the speed needed to compete at the college level.

Could I have done better? Absolutely. But I made a promise to God and myself to graduate with academic honors because I had eight siblings looking at the example I was setting with my academic performance. I also knew there were people doubting my academic prowess. Let it be understood, one's faith goes further than someone else's opinion.

The 1976–77 track and field season ended and I had to make a choice over the course of the summer. The choice I had to make was whether to continue participating on the track team at Shaw University, or just concentrate on being a student in order to reach my academic goals.

I left Raleigh, North Carolina, in the summer of 1977 without a job. Before I departed for Henderson, I applied for a job at United Parcel Service (UPS) just in case they needed employees during the summer, or when I returned to school. Two weeks after school ended, I went back home to find work and applied for a job with several factories. I chose to work for Southern Quilters, which paid a lousy hourly wage.

Southern Quilters was located less than five minutes from where I lived. Every day I worked for Southern, the same people I grew up with challenged me as to why I was working there.

For example, one of the supervisors knew my parents and family very well. He gave me a hard time on the job because I was considered "the college guy." What was I doing working at Southern Quilters taking their jobs? Even though the work was difficult, it wasn't the hardest work I had ever performed.

The supervisor I mentioned also had a reputation for assaulting people and that made the job tough as well. Had he threatened me, my uncles would have given him a hard time. My father was a no-nonsense type of man—he was known for defending his family no matter the circumstances.

We lived in the South and you simply had to defend yourself if you found yourself in a difficult situation. No one fooled around with my family when it came time for resolving misunderstandings. In the South, talk is cheap and a heavy dose of reality will follow if one disrespects your children. My parents asked me if I wanted to leave Southern Quilters and if so they would support my decision.

I picked up my check after completing three weeks of work and started working in our family grocery store. Two weeks after leaving the drudgery of factory work, I received a call from UPS in Raleigh. I only had to overcome one hurdle, and it was a lack of transportation. My father only had one car, so I talked to our next door neighbor. She was a widow and owned a car, but didn't know how to drive.

Our neighbor allowed me to drive her car until I could afford my own, so I commuted ninety miles each day to work at UPS. They paid $3.50 an hour plus benefits, which was better than the factory job I previously had.

I began working for UPS in July 1977, and worked there until October 1980, which meant I had to become even more disciplined and focused to balance my schoolwork with my part-time job at UPS. By the time I left UPS, I was earning over $12.50 an hour, plus benefits and paid holidays.

I began my sophomore year of college in August 1977 with

a new attitude because I had more certainty in my source of income. My grant and part-time job helped me make financial ends meet and allowed me to send money home to help my parents with my siblings.

Attending college on a full-time basis and working part-time wasn't easy, but no one ever said it would be. I paid my dues and was proud to take on the responsibility of being a student and wage earner. I learned more and more about myself once I organized my schedule, which included enrolling in classes, allotting sufficient time for rest, projecting the number of hours of study time I needed, and the number of hours I worked each month.

You have to know who you are when you have to make decisions that alter your life. I knew who I was when I went to class. I put in the quality time I needed to ensure that I would receive excellent grades. I knew who I was by prioritizing my life around my studies. If I had to make a decision to attend school or go to work, school always came first.

At the end of the first semester of my sophomore year, my grades were the best they had ever been, and I was going to ensure I maintained a high grade point average. I was beginning to take more of my core courses in business, which was great because I truly enjoyed business and accounting. I also decided to enroll in the Army Reserve Officer Training Corps Program (Army ROTC). I cross-enrolled at Saint Augustine's College, which was two miles from Shaw University, in order to find out if I could be all I could be as a soldier. I tossed around the idea and remained in the leadership course for a half semester, then realized it wasn't for me.

My Army ROTC course was coming along just great until the day we simulated a Claymore Mine. After the lab was over I informed the instructor I was going to complete the class; however, I was no longer interested in pursuing Army ROTC. At the end of the semester, I turned in my uniform and equipment.

My grades were very good at the end of the first semester of my sophomore year, and I was digging my heels in perfecting my study habits. I learned that one obtains more value studying by using the most under-used aspect of our daily lives, the library. If people took advantage of and used the library in their communities, they would learn so much more because the resources extend beyond the doors. The network of library resources is unlimited and can reach around the globe.

I was also getting acclimated to my job at UPS, and learning how to balance my school work and part-time job. It was paying dividends for me. The value of having a part-time job took the pressure off me because I didn't have to worry about money. It's strange how poverty traps people. I worried whether I could continue going to school, but once I got the job at UPS, everything fell into place.

Christmas break was great because my grades were good and I made the Dean's List. (I stayed on the Dean's List until I graduated.) I also decided to work a few double shifts at UPS. I was able to purchase gifts for my parents and siblings, and it made me proud to be able to make a contribution to my family and not be a burden to them.

My parents couldn't afford to contribute to my college tuition, and over the years the blessing came from the fact that I never needed money from them. I had faith in myself and knew I could make it—all I needed was a job, and I found the right one for me at UPS.

In the spring of 1978, I attended a speaking engagement at Shaw University by an individual named Dick Gregory. At the time, I did not understand what motivational speaking was all about. But when I look back at the eloquence of Mr. Gregory, I realize that he planted a seed for me in terms of entering the speaking industry.

Dick Gregory's mastery of the spoken language was unparalleled and I had never heard anyone speak the way he did. He talked about the amount of pressure women endure as a result of having their ears pierced, and what water does to the skin when people take a shower. I never forgot his speech because I had never heard an African-American that had a command of the English language the way Dick Gregory did. Other than Dr. Martin Luther King, I had never heard anyone speak so eloquently.

At the end of my sophomore year, I was expecting great things from myself from a grade perspective. I was not disappointed, because I received the highest grade point average since entering college. I really enjoyed college and knew who I was because I began to put more and more emphasis on my study habits.

Studying became fun for me, and anytime something becomes fun we tend to thrive. I not only thrived, I flourished. My sophomore year in college was coming to a close and I was looking forward to some down time, or so I thought.

The summer of 1978 was projected to be a scorcher. I wanted some relief from the heat and humidity at UPS. I had a classmate that cross-enrolled at North Carolina State University in order to attend the Air Force Reserve Officers Training Corps (AFROTC) program. Cadet Wells encouraged me to consider joining the program at North Carolina (N.C.) State University.

I scheduled a meeting with Lieutenant Colonel Mormino, AFROTC Commander at Detachment 595. Lieutenant Colonel Mormino explained how their program differed from the Army ROTC program, and then his staff gave me a tour of their facilities. I met some really nice people at N.C. State University.

Guess what happened to me? I signed up to attend an AFROTC basic camp in Dover, Delaware. I would not lose my job at UPS because they had to release me from work for six weeks because of the military. I didn't plan on joining the military—I just wanted to see what it was like, and besides, I would earn the same amount of money attending basic camp as I would have made working in the scorching heat in Raleigh that summer.

My parents were wondering what I was doing. I told them I had not lost my job but wanted to see whether I liked the Air Force. They understood once I explained it to them. In July 1978, I boarded a Greyhound bus to make the trip to Dover, Delaware.

I will never forget the bus ride to Dover because the driver stopped at a store in Virginia to pick up a package on the way to Delaware. I got off the bus to purchase a soda, and when I returned to the bus, the driver was driving away. What the driver didn't know is that I was on the track team and I was not going to let him drive off without me. Eventually, the bus driver stopped the bus to let me back on. I arrived in Dover, Delaware, and was picked up by Air Force personnel and driven to Dover Air Force Base.

To my wonderment, one of my high school classmates had enlisted in the Air Force and was assigned to Dover Air Force Base. I was going to have a great time because Jessie Gibbs, one of my high school classmates, had a car. This meant I could get a ride off base if I wanted to go into town.

Basic camp was a lot of fun and I had never flown on a plane before, so I would get my opportunity to ride one for the first time. However, first things first. After processing into basic camp, I was assigned a roommate by the name of Randall Mecham.

Randall was a fantastic guy from Valdosta, Georgia. We were friends from the very beginning of basic camp. We were assigned as roommates, which meant we were going to avoid demerits at all cost. Demerits were like discipline—if the inspector came to our room and found dust on the furniture, we would receive a demerit, which meant toilet cleaning duty or picking up paper on the weekend instead of having off-base privileges.

Randall and I kept our room clean, our military shoes spit shined, and the sheets on our beds nice and snug as required. The inspector could bounce a quarter off our beds. Our books had to be in the proper location in the room and the floors had to be shining—and they were.

Randall and I were both good runners; in fact, we were the fastest running tandem in the entire basic camp detachment. On any given day Randall or I were one of the two fastest runners at basic camp, and we were logging amazing times for the 1.5 mile run. In fact, my fastest time was six minutes and thirty-six seconds, which is fast.

At basic camp, I learned how to put on my uniform, spit shine my military shoes, and wear my flight cap. I learned how to march, and learned all of the courtesies associated with the military. I studied Air Force history and took tests to ensure that I learned my lessons. I didn't know how to swim when I arrived at basic camp and had to improvise when the water survival training exercise was conducted. Fortunately, everything worked out well.

Prior to arriving in Dover, I had never flown on a plane before. The second week of basic camp the entire detachment was scheduled to fly in the world's largest aircraft—a C-5. The C-5 is a cargo and troop mover; it is the length of a football field, and it can transport over seventy-three passengers in addition to the crew. It can also transport jet aircraft, tanks, and jeeps.

The Dover flight crew flew over Bermuda and I was a bit nervous because I couldn't really see that well. The plane only has a few windows, and as we continued to circle around the island, I was a bit sick. I survived the flight; however, it was only the beginning of my days flying all over the U.S. and halfway around the world. I love flying. I was about to realize a lifelong dream.

Basic camp was a great experience for me. It afforded me the opportunity to make a decision as to whether I would join the AFROTC program when I returned to Shaw University. During the fourth week of basic camp, our detachment was flown to Columbus Air Force Base in Columbus, Mississippi, for jet flight orientation.

If one is to truly understand aviation and what it's all about he must personally experience flying an Air Force jet. If you will recall, I mentioned earlier I always dreamt of flying. It was and continues to be my most consistent dream even to this day. August 1, 1978 was a day I will always remember because I was about to realize my dream of flying a jet aircraft.

After arriving aboard a C-5 aircraft from Dover, our entire detachment landed at Columbus Air Force Base in Mississippi for flight orientation. We were given flight suits to wear, so I donned my flight suit, boots, shades, and helmet. I was assigned to fly with Captain Gary Clay, a Columbus AFB Flight Instructor.

I greeted Captain Clay with a salute and then he briefly covered the flight plan with me. We boarded the T-37 aircraft, and while waiting for the air traffic controller to signal for take-off, Captain Clay told me to just relax. The control tower signaled us for take-off and away we went down the runway, at 140 miles an hour, and then we obtained lift. We were at one thousand, five thousand, then ten thousand feet in the air and it was one of those hot and humid Mississippi days.

Captain Clay spoke with the control tower and we leveled off at an altitude of ten thousand feet. After several minutes of communicating with the control tower, Captain Clay instructed me to take the stick and I did. Fortunately, our detachment had received a simulator ride prior to the flight orientation so we could understand the environment we were going to be in. I took the stick, flew the aircraft slightly to the right, then to the left, and leveled off again.

Then I heard Captain Clay state, "I want to show you some of the top gun maneuvers we conduct when we are training our pilots." By the time Captain Clay finished his sentence, we were flying upside down, then right side up. Then he banked the aircraft to the left, then to the right, and we leveled off again. After all of the banking Captain Clay conducted, I was praying aloud and it must have been funny to Captain Clay because he laughed and asked me if I was all right.

I told Captain Clay, "Yes I am all right; I just can't breathe." Captain Clay asked me whether I wanted to try a few more top gun maneuvers and I informed him that I had enough and would appreciate completing the flight. I had accomplished a lifelong goal of flying a jet aircraft. I realized during the flight that I would not become a pilot because I wore glasses and my vision didn't meet Air Force standards. I loved flying the Air Force jet, and would not trade the experience for anything.

Trust me—when you are flying an aircraft you have to know who you are because failure is not an option, and one mistake can be very unforgiving. I knew who I was after I successfully completed basic camp at Dover AFB. I met new people, who in many cases became lifelong friends. Most importantly, I learned to understand the military, specifically the Air Force way of life, while in basic camp. It would prove to be an experience that would lead to a career opportunity.

After returning to North Carolina in August 1978, I arrived just in time to begin my junior year of college at Shaw University. I discussed the basic camp experience with my parents and they were interested in what I had learned, but we never discussed whether I would join the AFROTC program at N.C. State.

I was finding my stride academically and looked for more intellectual challenges. I decided to attend the AFROTC meeting at N.C. State University. When I arrived at the N.C. State's campus I immediately went to speak with Lieutenant Colonel Mormino. He reviewed my records from basic camp and informed me that I should consider joining the program.

Shortly after departing my meeting with Colonel Mormino,

I hurried to my opportunity meeting and lo and behold! I ran into Gary Hamby, who also attended basic camp at Dover AFB. Gary and I greeted each other and headed to the meeting. I still hadn't decided on whether I would cross enroll at N.C. State for AFROTC up until the moment we were asked whether we wanted to join. Gary raised his hand to join the two-year program and so did I.

Gary and I laughed at each other because he knew I had not planned on joining, so he came to me afterwards to discuss it. I said, "Gary, when I saw your hand go up in the air I had to join because we can have fun like we did at Dover AFB." Deep down inside I wasn't sure if I was making the right decision because I didn't have any knowledge to fall back on. No one in my immediate family had served in the military. In retrospect, I made what proved to be a very career defining decision, as you will find out later.

After Colonel Mormino's staff reviewed my grades, they offered me a two-year Air Force scholarship. I considered accepting the AFROTC scholarship for a week or so; however, I declined. I declined the scholarship because I still had an opportunity to opt out of serving the military once I graduated. I did not take joining the military lightly when I was in college because I didn't want to get caught up in a war I knew nothing about. I was still trying to reconcile the Vietnam War issues.

My parents purchased their first television in 1967, and I remember to this day watching Walter Cronkite report on the war. I can still see Mr. Cronkite reporting on the number of casualties that occurred each day. I am sure our youth today are going through what I went through trying to understand the meaning of war and casualties, it's very complex.

I will never forget how bad it made me feel listening to the casualty reports. I didn't understand why people were killing each other; it didn't make any sense to me. Please understand I was only nine years of age when I saw and heard the events that took place during the Vietnam War. I wish someone could have explained it to me. In many ways, I didn't understand war during that stage of my life, primarily because I believed people should work out their differences before they start destroying each other.

The bottom line is that I examined myself before I made the decision to join the AFROTC program at N.C. State University. I will tell anyone contemplating joining the military to examine themselves before they sign up. I reconciled deep-rooted issues within myself, and signed on the dotted line.

There were a couple of fascinating men at N.C. State University that I followed over the course of my career. One of them was football coach Lou Holtz. The other was basketball coach Norm Sloan. It's amazing how you come in contact with great people. I was a fan of N.C. State's athletic program, and during the summer I would visit the campus to play basketball against N.C. State Wolfpack basketball players.

Oftentimes N.C. State players would underestimate my game for one reason or another. They didn't know I had been a track and field athlete, which meant they couldn't out run me. They didn't like anyone out-playing them, but my friends and I did on numerous occasions.

I was taking a full load of classes during the first half of my junior year. I had to become even more disciplined since I also had to drive to N.C. State's campus and factor my AFROTC classes into my schedule. In my junior year, I realized I was going to accomplish my goal of graduating from college. The impact of me graduating from college would make a positive impact on my family.

At the end of the first semester of my junior year, I made the Dean's List again and was well on my way to reaching my goal of academic excellence. AFROTC was working out just great for me as well. I became the flight commander for the sophomores. I was a cadet Captain at the time, and we were scheduled for an inspection by none other than my good friend, Cadet Major Gary Hamby.

It was my first inspection as an AFROTC cadet. I got in my car and drove the two miles from Shaw University to the N.C. State University campus. I put my uniform on in the restroom and headed straight to the athletic field where the inspection was to take place.

My cadet flight was in place and properly aligned as we had discussed at practice. We were ready for this inspection. Gary made his way to my flight and began his inspection. Then he approached me. We saluted each other, and he informed me that my entire flight of cadets had their belt buckles on backwards.

Gary proceeded to inspect my uniform and then we both realized I had my belt buckle on incorrectly. Gary looked at me and I looked at him and we both started laughing because my cadets had their belt buckles on correctly. I was the one that had my uniform on incorrectly. To this day, whenever Gary and I see each other, we always talk about the inspection.

The semester was coming to a close and Christmas of 1978 was upon us. I decided to work double, and in some cases triple, shifts to earn extra money so I could give my mother and father nice gifts for the holidays. I also purchased gifts for my grandmothers and siblings. It was good being home for a couple of days during the holidays, and then I had to return to Raleigh.

UPS was up and running for the entire holiday season and I was promoted from loading trucks to sorting, which is easier on the body. Working at UPS kept me in good physical shape because it was a demanding job; even though it was part-time, I had to achieve balance between my schoolwork and my job.

In the spring of 1979, I came out of the gate rolling because I was enrolled in my core courses in business at Shaw University, and was doing very well. Tuition rates were going up, which meant I was coming up short on my tuition. I was able to work with the financial aid office to reconcile the shortfall.

Close call to say the least, my Pell Grant was still keeping my head above water and my part-time job pulled me through my financial crisis. I never took my academics for granted while in school. A number of my classmates didn't have a job and had to return home.

At the end of my junior year I was sitting on cloud nine because my grades were very good and I made the Dean's List once again. This positioned me nicely for my senior year of college. I enrolled in summer school at Saint Augustine's College and took an accounting class in order to lighten my course load heading into my senior year.

My first year of AFROTC was proving to be invaluable because of the leadership courses I was taking. I was also selected to attend the Third Lieutenant Program, an Air Force sponsored program that allowed cadets to spend two weeks on an Air Force Base to discuss what it's like to be on active duty. After summer school ended, I flew to Champaign, Illinois, to participate in the program hosted by officers in my chosen career field. I had chosen the comptroller career field, which included budgeting, accounting, financial management, and cost analysis or auditing.

The Third Lieutenant Program sealed the deal for me in terms of helping me make the decision to accept a commission upon graduating from Shaw University. Chanute Air Force Base was located near the University of Illinois and Peoria, which for me was the windiest city I had ever visited.

After the two-week Third Lieutenant program ended, I took a commuter aircraft from Champaign to connect in Chicago, and tragedy struck. Fortunately, I had flown on a plane before — otherwise I would have gotten sick because the small commuter aircraft I was flying on continued to circle O'Hare Airport.

A plane bound for Los Angeles crashed, and all aircraft were in a holding pattern until the ground crew could clean up the wreckage. I was very nervous; however, my connecting flight took off and landed in Raleigh without a hitch. I prayed a lot before, during, and after the flight.

After returning to campus to begin my senior year at Shaw University, I was very confident I was going to graduate on time. I visited the AFROTC Detachment at N.C. State University and discussed the Third Lieutenant Program with the detachment commander and my peers.

Prior to departing I was asked whether I would like to become the Cadet Corps Commander and I must admit it was very tempting. However, I knew the responsibilities that went with leading over three hundred cadets could offset my graduation. I humbly turned down the opportunity because my grades and my part-time job at UPS were intertwined.

Even though I received a stipend of one hundred dollars per month from AFROTC, which helped me make ends meet, I maintained my focus on graduating from college and the impact it would have on my younger siblings. If the cycle of poverty was going to be broken, it would come through me. I had been promoted to Cadet Major in my senior year of college and I was in line to be offered a commission as a second lieutenant in the United States Air Force.

By the way, I was the only student at Shaw University enrolled in AFROTC during my senior year. The Army ROTC cadets at Shaw were enrolled at Saint Augustine's College and there were at least twelve seniors projected to receive a commission.

Christmas break came and went and UPS was keeping my finances in order as I headed into the last semester of my senior year. I hit the books really hard and was on track to receive a good grade point average to close out my undergraduate career.

The Air Force was primed to offer me a commission and I was ready for graduation day, which was May 10th 1980. The only thing I was preparing for was the number of family members who would attend.

My mother was going to be attending my graduation ceremony, along with my sisters, Jackie and Gloria Jean. My Aunt Carrie Marable would also attend, along with my cousin Shelton McKnight and his family members. After contacting my father, unfortunately he was unable to attend. School officials and my friends wanted to meet my father to compliment him on my academic achievements. I suppose he just wasn't meant to be there.

May 10th was a beautiful day in Raleigh. I wore my AFROTC uniform under my cap and gown. As the convocation center filled to capacity, I was able to spot my family. I saw my mother waving, and I waved back at her. I was proud of my family and wanted to share my achievement with them. After all, my guidance counselor had told me I didn't have what it takes to get accepted to college or to be a successful college student. So much for personal opinions.

As the President of Shaw University called my name, I walked across the stage, shook his hand and thanked him for supporting me over the entire four years of school. As he called my name he stated, "Paul L. Vann is receiving his bachelor's degree in business management and is graduating Cum Laude." People attending the graduation ceremony enthusiastically applauded me for my academic accomplishments. I looked at my mother, and she was in tears because she knew I could do it. I was as happy for her as I was for myself because I could not have done it without the love and support of her and my entire family.

In other words, when I received my bachelors degree on May 10th, so did my parents and my siblings because no one ever achieves anything without the support and help of others. I was proud of myself because I was not a burden on my parents; I helped them financially so they could help my siblings make it once they graduated from high school.

My day wasn't done. After all of the degrees were awarded, all students receiving commissions to serve in the military were lined up to receive their orders. All of the Army ROTC cadets went ahead of me because the Army is the oldest service; thus they went first.

Air Force representatives from N.C. State University were up next. They called my name and stated, "Paul Lawrence Vann, having completed all academic requirements for commissioning to become a second lieutenant in the United States Air Force after repeating the oath will be a second lieutenant in the Air Force." I repeated the oath as required by law, saluted the officer, and shook his hand.

As a result of completing the Air Force ROTC program and the academic requirements for a degree, it was acknowledged I had demonstrated a high degree of ability, initiative, and other leadership qualities essential to successful performance of duty as an Air Force officer. I was also designated a Distinguished Graduate of Air Force ROTC.

The Air Force officer pinned the second lieutenant bars on my uniform and I walked across the stage. The entire convocation center gave me a standing ovation. I was in tears because I saw my mother crying her eyes out from joy, and all I could think of was her commenting that I was a blessing to our family.

It took four years to arrive at my graduation date of May 10, 1980. My graduation date will always will be a special day for me, but more important, it is special for my family. The result of me graduating from high school and four years later from college influenced my siblings. For example, all eight of my brothers and sisters graduated from high school. All three of my brothers received bachelor's degrees and two of them received master's degrees. I earned two master's degrees over the course of my military career. My sisters attended community college and most of them work in the medical field, while others work in the franchise industry.

My parents were proud of all of their children. When you consider the fact that neither of my parents received their high school diploma, nor their parents before them, one can now see just how important education is to our family. Education pulled us out of the grips of poverty. Even though my family knows what poverty looks like, we also know God has a hand in the upward progression of our family, and we had no doubts we would be able to turn it around.

Having the faith of a mustard seed is important when it comes to overcoming poverty. That's why I say you have to know who you are, otherwise you will be swayed by any wind of doctrine.

ACTION PLAN #1

Believe in Yourself

IT'S IMPORTANT NOT ONLY TO BELIEVE IN YOURSELF, BUT ALSO to believe in something greater than yourself. What do I mean by believing in something greater than yourself? It's quite simple. When we believe in something greater than ourselves, it's possible for each of us to stretch beyond our current limitations. If a Marine, soldier, airman, or sailor decides his or her goal is to become Chairman of the Joint Chiefs of Staff (CJCS), they can achieve this lofty goal. The position of the CJCS is greater than the Chairman occupying the position. Please note, there will be people lined up to tell you it's impossible to become CJCS; however, if we really believe in ourselves it can happen.

Please write down seven things that lets you know who you are. It may have been a new challenge, new military assignment, or new leadership. It's okay to think outside the box because this exercise focuses on our convictions and commitment to our future success.

1. _____

2. _____

3. _____

4. _____

5. _____

6. _____

7. _____

I did not, nor did my parents, have money for me to attend college. Instead of sitting out a year to earn money to attend college, I decided to take a summer job and earned enough money to make it through the first year. Fortunately for me, I received a grant to help me achieve my goal and I graduated four years later.

Deep down inside, I knew I had to motivate myself to defeat failure. Failure is the natural enemy of success; however, through the power of motivation we can overcome any challenges that come our way. Remain steadfast and immovable when following your dreams. If you know who you are, you will succeed.

ACTION PLAN #2

Converting Our Internal Conversation into Positive Dialogue

STUDIES HAVE SHOWN THAT PURE SILENCE DOES NOT EXIST IN the world. What do I mean by the aforementioned statement? Mother Earth in all of her beauty hums; people also hum. Those moments we consider serene, peaceful, and quiet actually consist of a humming sound. Take advantage of the humming sound and fill it with positive thoughts and positive ideas to transform your dreams into reality.

It's my belief when we experience silence and tranquility we should fill it with positive affirmations. Remember when you are in the midst of a storm, peace is within you. Please list five affirmations that bring you tranquility.

1. _____

2. _____

3. _____

4. _____

5. _____

Finding Our Center

Now that you've listed your affirmations, let's concentrate on our center. We all have a center, so let's work to connect or reconnect with our center at this point. How does your favorite affirmation relate to your peace of mind? It has been said that peace of mind is wealth; in other words, by having peace of mind we defeat stress wherever it exists because we are conscious of its presence. All military personnel have a center.

After discovering your center, please describe what gives you peace of mind._____

_____

_____

While on vacation in Aruba a few years ago, I decided to participate in parasailing. I never attempted parasailing before; however, I thought it would be a lot of fun. The crew driving the speed boat connected me to the parachute that supported me while parasailing. Minutes later, I was launched off the back of the boat into the sky. I ascended one, two, three, and then four stories high. I could see the entire island and thought this is what it must be like to be a bird. My parasailing experience made me realize I had peace of mind because of the tranquility I experienced. I parasail as often as I can. What fills your parachute and gives you peace of mind?_____

_____

_____

*"Unlimited possibilities await the person
who never stops striving to reach success."*
—Paul Lawrence Vann

~ 3 ~

Living on Higher Ground

To anyone who is looking for success or happiness
I say believe in yourself, have faith in your abilities.
—Dr. Norman Vincent Peale

IN MAY 1980 I WAS ON CLOUD NINE AFTER RECEIVING MY FIRST
military assignment orders. I was going to be assigned to Los
Angeles Air Force Station, which meant I was going to be living
in L.A. to work as a financial analyst. I told my parents and siblings about it and they were happy for me. I had spoken with my
best friend Bryant McKnight and he agreed to drive with me to
L.A. in October 1980.

In June 1980, I received a phone call from an Air Force assignments officer, instructing me that my orders for Los Angeles Air
Force Station had been revoked because the personnel require-
ment at WPAFB was more pressing than at L.A. Air Station. I'll
never forget what she said, "Lieutenant Vann, your orders for
assignment to Los Angeles Air Force Station have been revoked.
Your new set of orders is forthcoming for your assignment to
Wright-Patterson Air Force Base in Dayton, Ohio."

The Air Force assignments office turned my world upside-
down because I pictured myself in Hollywood—with television
and movie stars—and on the beach looking at the Pacific Ocean.
I already decided to attend the University of Southern California
to earn my master's degree in business. I had also determined I
would only stay in the Air Force for four years and become an

actor. How was I going to do this from Dayton, Ohio?

The Air Force gave me five months to report to Wright-Patterson Air Force Base for my first military assignment. I remained in Raleigh, North Carolina after graduating from college, and continued to work part-time with UPS. By the time I departed for military duty, I had worked at UPS for a total of three years and three months. They played an instrumental role in my collegiate success, and I will always be thankful for their support.

The summer of 1980 brought tragedy to the McKnight family, and it changed my view of my community as well. I drove my Great Aunt Carrie Marable to a family reunion in New York on the Hudson River. Aunt Carrie requested that I drive her to Long Island to stay with relatives on my mother's side of the family. Francine and William Earl Hawkins lived in Brentwood, New York, and had a very beautiful home. Francine and William Earl lived very comfortably on Long Island. Their lifestyle convinced me and reinforced the reality that my family was in more poverty than I realized.

The drive to New York was hilarious. After I had driven the first nineteen miles from our home in Henderson to the Virginia border on I-85 north, Aunt Carrie told me I was driving too fast. The maximum speed limit in 1980 was fifty-five miles per hour. I was driving between sixty and sixty-two miles per hour, and she scolded me for driving too fast. We made it safely to Long Island; however, it seemed as though it took two days for what should have been a ten-hour drive.

Cousin William Earl Hawkins and his wife Francine welcomed Aunt Carrie and me into their home, and I immediately called home to let my parents know we had arrived safely. I heard what turned out to be the worst news I would hear all summer. My father told me Bryant McKnight had been killed. Bryant McKnight was like a brother to me. When we were pre-teens, our parents' homes were located side-by-side prior to us moving to 340 Skenes Avenue.

What was more alarming to me was that someone in my community had murdered Bryant because he was defending his cousin, whom someone had threatened. After the altercation, he was standing with his cousin in their yard and the fellow he had the altercation with returned in a car and pretended to apologize. When they attempted to forgive one another, the young man took his gun and shot Bryant in the head. I will never forget what happened to my best friend Bryant. He was only twenty-one. I remember the dreaded evening my father informed me of this tragedy.

After hearing about Bryant, I didn't want to attend the family reunion, but I did anyway because it helped to be around family at the time. Aunt Carrie and I returned to Henderson on Sunday evening and I went to see the McKnight family and offered my sympathy and condolences.

Our entire community attended Bryant's funeral and we all paid our respects to this military veteran at Welcome Chapel Baptist Church in Henderson. Personally, I changed after Bryant was killed. I was going into the future without my Aunt Carolyn and now my best friend Bryant. I was sick and tired of being sick and tired about black-on-black crime and the devastating impact it has on families and friends. Enough is truly enough and I was not going to trust many people any more. I didn't plan on getting to close to anyone because it's tough when tragedy strikes and you lose them.

I began to put myself back together again after throwing myself into a consistent prayer life because I knew I had the ultimate challenge ahead of me with my Air Force commitment. I contacted my sponsor at Wright-Patterson AFB and he informed me I was due to report to his office on October 15, 1980.

Prior to departing to Dayton, I finished my last week at UPS and my friends and supervisors threw me a party at the Pizza Inn near the Raleigh hub. I really enjoyed my experience at UPS because I had a lot of friends there and they were down to earth and laid-back people. I knew I would never see a lot of them again, and my premonition was correct.

I left Raleigh, North Carolina, on October 13, 1980, and drove to Henderson to see my family prior to departing. I spent a day talking with my mother and father and siblings. I thanked them for supporting me during my college years, and had an extended meeting with my younger siblings to inspire them to do their best to support our parents. I told them if they needed me, all they had to do was call me.

On the morning of October 14, I kissed and hugged my mother and told her good bye, and told her that I loved her and would be contacting her on a regular basis. I talked to my father and told him I loved him and to take care of everyone and not to worry about me because I would be just fine.

Then I stopped to see both of my grandmothers. I hugged and kissed them. We knew I was on to something great by me finishing college and serving in the Air Force. They told me they knew I was going to be the one to help bring our family out of poverty and into prosperity. I told my grandmothers not to worry because I was on a mission to be successful and I meant every word I spoke.

I drove back to Raleigh to meet the movers at my apartment, and they picked up the few items I possessed. I packed the remaining essentials in my car and on October 15, 1980, I drove from Raleigh, North Carolina to Dayton, Ohio. After arriving at Wright-Patterson Air Force Base (AFB), I knew I was going to make a difference in the Air Force because I didn't come all the way to Ohio to waste my time. I came to "Aim High," just as the Air Force motto stated.

My assignment sponsor informed me I was assigned to the Aeronautical Systems Division, Reconnaissance Warfare System Program Office or (ASD/RW). This is but one of many acronyms I will be using throughout this chapter. In other words, I was going to be an acquisition cost estimator and financial analyst for aircraft aeronautical equipment, which meant I would be performing and conducting financial analysis and cost estimates on acquisition programs.

I was fortunate to discover there were a lot of junior officers (newly commissioned lieutenants) assigned to Wright-Patterson AFB. It was the place to be because the large acquisition budgets meant there were plenty of opportunities available. Wright-Patterson AFB also had a stellar line-up of general officers and civilians who knew the acquisition arena as well, and could groom young officers along the way.

My supervisor's name was Martin Zydell. He was a civil servant and a veteran who attained the rank of Captain while in the Air Force. After in-processing at Wright-Patterson, I immediately purchased my uniforms, set up my bank account, and conducted an apartment search. The one thing I realized right off the bat was the difference in weather between North Carolina and Ohio; it was much colder in Ohio than I realized.

I almost froze on my first day of military duty because there had been a run on uniform jackets at the base clothing store. I was thinking about California even more, but after attending my first orientation meeting with other young officers assigned to Wright-Patterson, I knew I would enjoy my first assignment in the Air Force.

After speaking to Mr. Zydell, I informed him of my intentions to earn a master's degree, and he encouraged me to do so. After reviewing the school availability list, I selected Central Michigan University (CMU) to work towards a business administration degree. CMU offered satellite classes every Friday evening through Saturday afternoon.

I was to become the first person in my family to earn a master's degree; thus, I went back to my study mode. I attended school on a part-time basis so I could learn my job responsibilities and duties in the Reconnaissance Warfare System Program Office.

Even though my initial military orders were revoked, I understood being assigned to Wright-Patterson AFB offered me the best opportunity as a young military officer. I was given an opportunity to learn about the all-important defense contracting and acquisition arena. Many of the general officers I met while assigned to the Aeronautical Systems Division were great leaders as well as great people.

Prior to military duty at Wright-Patterson, I had never met an African-American general officer. My personal experience growing up was very limited when it came to African-Americans in high-level leadership positions. Outside of African-American pastors in church, my exposure to other leaders was very limited.

In May 1981, General Titus Hall took command and became Deputy for Reconnaissance and Electronic Warfare Systems, Headquarters Aeronautical Systems Division, Wright-Patterson Air Force Base. I was very fortunate to work under the leadership of Brigadier General Titus Hall because it gave me an opportunity to observe an African-American in a leadership position. He was a great role model for me, and his presence made a tremendous impact on my career and my life. I am confident other young African-American officers at Wright-Patterson AFB had the same impression of Brigadier General Hall.

My initial project assignments consisted of conducting detailed cost performance analysis on multimillion-dollar electronic warfare programs. I also performed cost estimates in support of contracts upwards of five hundred million dollars. Working with big government contracts helped me gain valuable insight into the business world, which played a key role in me considering working in private industry in the future.

It was a blessing to have my first officer performance report endorsed by Brigadier General Hall. This was a big deal because junior officers rarely received high level endorsements from a general officer.

I will tell anyone that joins the military—whether in the enlisted or officer ranks—you will be given unlimited opportunities to learn. The first thing the Air Force did for me was to schedule numerous career or specialty classes to help me learn about my career field as soon as possible. I balanced my master's degree program with the cost and budget analysis classes, along with the practical experience I attained on the job.

One needs to understand over the course of my military career I did not like the Air Force; I loved the Air Force because they believed in the whole-person concept. The key to succeeding in the Air Force was to give your all and be an asset to your team, and in my case to my system program office (SPO)—which was the Aeronautical Systems Division/Reconnaissance Warfare System Program Office (ASD/RW).

The Air Force is about teamwork. I believe my decision to play football in high school and participate on the track team played an instrumental role in me being able to make the adjustment from college to a career in the Air Force. To be successful in the Air Force requires discipline and the desire to learn as much as you possibly can about leadership.

It is very apparent the mission of the Air Force is to fly, fight, and win in combat if called upon. I learned early on that my assignment at Wright-Patterson AFB was a blessing from God and I no longer thought about the assignment to Los Angeles. Even though I did not have wings to become a pilot or navigator, I was allowed to play a pivotal role in helping our pilots do their jobs better by conducting analysis and pricing the electronic equipment that they needed to perform their duties effectively.

By working with defense contractors such as TRW, Sanders Associates, and subcontractors such as AT&T, I was able to get a bird's eye view of how the defense acquisition process worked. As a cost analyst supporting over seven different programs, I took the initiative to work closely with ASD/RW program managers, logistics specialists and contracting officers. This broadened my knowledge base considerably.

I highly recommend a career in the U.S. Air Force as well as one of the other outstanding branches of the military because it is an outstanding way to serve this great country we live in. As the current Air Force motto states, "Come Into the Blue."

On October 16, 1982, I was promoted to the rank of First Lieutenant in the Air Force. I was well on my way to becoming a more valuable asset to the Air Force and to my country. My parents were proud of my accomplishments, and I was more motivated to achieve even greater rewards as my career looked brighter and brighter.

After a year on my Air Force assignment, it was time for my apartment lease to expire. I had the fortune to meet and become close friends with an officer by the name of Cliff Frye, who was a program manager at ASD/RW. Cliff was a fellow North Carolinian and he's one of the brightest people I know; he and I started our tour about the same time and hit it off as friends.

Cliff and I were roommates for roughly two years prior to me receiving a new assignment. Cliff and I decided to lease a house from a civilian named Frank Tuck.

Frank became a member of the Senior Executive Service (SES) in the federal government. He's a brilliant man and an individual I have always admired. Frank was a role model for many young officers.

My experience growing up in Henderson, North Carolina, didn't provide me with the exposure to see outstanding men like Frank Tuck in high-level leadership positions. I have admiration for Frank because you had to be better than good to perform program-management related work at Wright-Patterson.

Frank is married to Dorothy, and they are two of my favorite people because they were both good at what they did in their professions. Oftentimes observation is a positive motivator and when I think of role models, Frank and Dorothy come to mind very quickly.

There are so many great people I met at Wright-Patterson that are still friends. One of the first people I met was Darrel Edwards. The first apartment I moved into was on Woodman Park Drive, and one of the first people I met at the apartment complex was Darrel. I knew we would be friends for life, and we are to this day. Darrel and I were earning our master's degrees at Central Michigan University and we had high career aspirations in the early 1980s. We had the vision to see into the future, and knew that advancing in our prospective fields would require advanced degrees. We both earned our degrees.

One night Darrel called me and said, "I am getting married." I said, "How can you get married when you are not dating anyone?" We laughed and I knew he had met Diane, who is a beautiful lady. They got married and are wonderful people. Recently, Darrel and Diane were in Washington, DC during the summer with their two children. My wife, daughter and I visited with them and we were both happy to see each other and our families together after twenty long years.

Daarel Burnett is another individual I met. He was a year ahead of me in entering the Air Force. Daarel graduated from Morehouse College and was a very dynamic officer who was doing fabulous things at the B-1 System Program Office. We were in the same career field and shared notes about career goals and aspirations. Daarel and I also played on two base basketball championship teams at Wright-Patterson, and have the trophies to prove it. Daarel retired from the Air Force. He and his wife Colette reside in the Dayton, Ohio area.

Linda James was a year behind me entering the Air Force. Linda was a beautiful lady from Miami, Florida. Linda also was in the comptroller career field and she went on to do great things in the Air Force. She was assigned to the Pentagon for a number of years. Linda has since retired and her family resides in the Washington, DC metropolitan area.

Claude Jones graduated from Shaw University a year before I did. Upon arriving at Wright-Patterson, I discovered he was enrolled and was earning his master's degree in aeronautical engineering from the Air Force Institute of Technology. This man is brilliant and he and his wife Linda are like family to me. They have two children and reside in the Washington, DC metropolitan area.

While the list of people I mentioned earlier is not inclusive, I would like to name a few people to say thanks for sharing the experience at Wright-Patterson: Brian Marshall, Nathan and Holly Krekula, Phil Perry, Doc Warr, Darrel Moody, Dave Hubah, Dave Pyant, Cesar Sharper, Paula Sharper, Mike Vila, Kathy Campbell, Don Campbell, Don Walters, Ken Lai, John Allen, Stan Ritchie, Roger Leath, John Phillips, Dario Ramirez, Launna Cuffy and Diane Armon, Steve Shackleford and the rest of the fabulous people who served a grateful nation at Wright-Patterson AFB.

Three years into my first assignment, I began performing cost performance work. This entailed visiting defense contractor facilities throughout the United States to evaluate their management control systems. As team chief, I directed a staff of four officers. We analyzed contractor budgets, schedules, reporting information, management and staff. We provided detailed reports to the System Program Office (SPO) Director.

A typical temporary duty assignment consisted of departing Dayton, Ohio, fly to Chicago to work for two days, and then flying to Boston and New Hampshire to work for three days, and flying directly to Los Angeles to work with the prime contractor for a week. This trip would consist of two consecutive weeks of work and travel, resulting in a thorough report for the SPO Director.

I loved the travel because you can learn so much more by visiting the contractor facilities. You could touch and see the equipment being developed and discuss ways to make the acquisition process work more efficiently, thereby saving our government and taxpayers money.

Our main objective was to ensure the contractor was living up to his end of the contractual agreement, and we were pleased to find they do excellent work as long as we remain engaged throughout the process. I enjoyed the programs at ASD/RW and would not trade the experience for anything in the world.

Another great aspect of being assigned to Wright-Patterson was the opportunity to volunteer for various committee activities. Extracurricular volunteer activities for me included serving as a tour guide for ROTC cadets from area universities, working on the Black History Month Committee, and working as a volunteer for the American Red Cross at Wright-Patterson Medical Center. Competing on the base softball, flag football, and basketball teams were positive activities because competing and winning the base championship helped maintain morale in our organization.

In 1983 I received the Outstanding Young Man of America Award in recognition of outstanding professional achievement, superior leadership ability, and exceptional service to the community. I was honored to receive the award and it was a testament to the opportunities I was given by my leadership and the positive environment I was working in.

I visited my parents on the holidays while on vacation (leave). Henderson, North Carolina was a twelve-hour drive from Dayton, Ohio, so my roommate Cliff and I took shifts driving. I was always thrilled to see my family and to share my experience with them and my siblings.

My younger siblings were progressing well in their school-work and it seemed like each year another child in the Vann family was graduating from high school. I was very proud of my brothers and sisters because they did their best in school and it showed when graduation time rolled around.

My mother's health was of concern to all of my family members. On a temporary duty assignment to Los Angeles, I decided to take a trip to Las Vegas with some friends of mine. I called home to speak to my mother and she didn't sound like herself, but she wouldn't tell anyone what was going on. Over time we discovered that she was losing blood; however, she wouldn't tell anyone she was suffering. Finally our family doctor discovered it during an examination. My mother was having heart problems. She was fortunate it was caught in the early stages. We were keeping a watchful eye on mom and praying to the Lord.

Dad's health was also visibly failing. My father was having early signs of Parkinson's Disease, and he also had high blood pressure and diabetes. Our father was in a risk group for everything. We were praying for his health to improve as well.

I continued to be actively involved in church after moving to Dayton. The pastor of the church I joined was from Henderson. This supported my belief that my assignment was by no means happen chance; in other words, I was meant to be living in Dayton. I led young adults' Sunday school at church, and led prayers during the worship service. We must all remember to pray for our parents before they become ill, and for ourselves so we can remain strong during a physical setback.

I met an individual by the name of Ken Lai in my master's degree program at Central Michigan University. Ken was a former Mr. Ohio and knew all the renowned body builders like Arnold Schwarzenegger and Lou Ferrigno. Ken was a native Hawaiian and was a great guy. We became fast friends.

One weekend I noticed Ken was absent from class. I asked the professor if he had heard anything from Ken and he said no. I contacted Ken's wife, Susan, and she informed me that Ken was in serious condition in the hospital. I immediately drove to the hospital and when I arrived, I didn't recognize him. Ken Lai was six feet two inches tall with muscles bulging out of his shirt, but he had lost over fifty pounds after being diagnosed with colon cancer. Ken lost all of his hair and was a mere shadow of himself, and I was sad. I prayed for Ken on the spot and he looked at me with his great smile and said, "Paul, be careful of the foods you eat—it caused the colon cancer I have."

I immediately thought about my best friend Bryant McKnight because I was about to lose another great friend. Ken lived a few years longer; however, I contacted his wife and she informed me that he had in fact passed away. Another warrior has gone to heaven, my Lord.

In June 1984, Martin (Marty) Zydell was my supervisor, and he informed me that I had received a regular appointment in the Air Force. What does this mean? A regular appointment in the military is the equivalent of an academy appointment. It gives the selectee the option to retire at thirty years of service. It can be an advantage when meeting promotion boards and competing for promotions with my contemporaries.

Proud is the word that comes to mind when I reflect on the wonderful events that took place during my initial military assignment at Wright-Patterson AFB. In early 1984, I applied for and was selected to attend the Education With Industry (EWI) Program sponsored by the Air Force Institute of Technology.

The Air Force Institute of Technology (AFIT) was one of the most demanding schools in America. I was very fortunate to discover programs such as EWI because every experience helped me to grow professionally and personally.

EWI was a ten-month program for junior officers that

allowed them to work for a company to learn the intricacies of private industry. I worked for National Data Corporation (NDC) located in Atlanta, Georgia. I supported their accounting department. I learned state tax accounting, conducted payroll analysis, and helped develop an automated customer tracking system, which assisted with point of sales management for NDC.

I began my EWI assignment in September 1984, and completed the program in June 1985. The managers at NDC were wonderful people. An individual by the name of Turner Carter was an accountant for NDC and a Morehouse graduate. Turner is a great man and he and his wife Patricia are great people. The Carter's have two children and currently reside in the Atlanta metropolitan area. I have great admiration for the Carters because they exemplify what two people with determination can do to raise a wonderful family.

My first impressions of Atlanta were not very good. After three months, though, I was beginning to enjoy Atlanta more and more. When I arrived in Atlanta the population was less than a million people; now it's a sprawling metropolis. It's also the home of Dr. Martin Luther King, Jr. He was a great man and even though he is no longer with us I still consider him to be one of the most influential people the world has ever known. The world could use some of Dr. King's wisdom today.

Exactly four years after entering the Air Force, during my EWI assignment in Atlanta, I was promoted to Captain. I celebrated my promotion with some of my family members living in Atlanta. My cousin Cheryl and her husband Steve Bacon and Cynthia Hicks had been living in Atlanta a few years prior to me being assigned there. Steve and I are fraternity (Kappa Alpha Psi) brothers so we have a lot in common.

ACTION PLAN #1

Aim High, Then Higher, to Achieve Excellence

WHAT PRICE ARE YOU WILLING TO PAY TO ACHIEVE SUCCESS? It's been said time and again if we are to achieve success, we must have a burning desire to make our dreams become reality. We must aim high, then higher, to achieve excellence in our field of expertise in the military. We become experts in our professions because we give consideration to every single detail. We know our contribution to national defense is vital to our nation's success.

If we confront enemies foreign or domestic, we are more than prepared to defend our freedom, liberty, and way of life because we are united. We achieve higher levels of excellence in defense of America because we put our best team (Army, Navy, Marines, Air Force, Guard and Reserves, and Coast Guard) in the theater of war. We can't lose.

Please write down five things you can do to make our team better. It could be coordinating amongst the different services. Consider morale boosters. Strive to be the best you can be through unity of mission.

1. _____

2. _____

3. _____

4. _____

5. _____

Over the years we meet a lot of people professionally and personally. The quality of our relationships speaks volumes about us. It's very important to cultivate strong professional relationships because in life we tend to see people we met when we first joined the military. In order to be effective at networking, first find our how you can help someone. Odds are the people you help will be willing to help you as well.

How many of us are willing to learn something new? Successful people never stop learning; in fact they accelerate their learning according to their weaknesses. Show me a person who knows it all, and I will show you a person who is a failure. It's imperative for us to manage our success and we do this by actively researching and learning as much as we can about the functional area we select as our calling.

ACTION PLAN #2

I Believe I Can Fly!

DID YOU KNOW THAT YOU CAN FLY? I KNOW THIS STATEMENT sounds strange, but we can achieve whatever we believe. Prior to attending an Air Force basic camp I had never flown on an airplane before. Four weeks into basic camp I was flying a T-37 aircraft. The U.S. Air Force flew cadets from Dover Air Force Base in Delaware to Columbus Air Force Base in Mississippi as part of our basic camp experience. I flew an Air Force jet as part of my flight orientation. Though I did not become a pilot, I will always be able to say I flew an Air Force jet.

I believe you can also fly! Perhaps not a jet aircraft, but you can fly in your branch of the military or field of endeavor. What do you wish to achieve in your life and how do you see yourself after achieving your goal? Please list five things you plan to achieve that will help you fly in your field of expertise.

1. _____

2. _____

3. _____

4. _____

5. _____

Going Up into the Wild Blue Yonder and Beyond

In order to be the best in our fields of endeavor we must change our thoughts. Our thoughts drive our actions; thus, we must believe we are the best at what we do. Believing we are the best at what we do does not mean we are better than anyone else; it simply means we are just as good. Going up into the wild blue yonder and beyond denotes we are going to the next level of our greatness.

What defines your next level of greatness?_____

_____

_____

We know we have reached our next level of greatness when achieving excellence becomes second nature. In other words, we no longer wonder if we are going to excel; we simply do. Going up into the wild blue yonder and beyond is an experience like no other, and for me, working with a team or group of people on high-level military programs and projects lets me know I am making a difference. I knew I was making a difference in the military after being invited to the White House for a dinner. Need I say more?

~ 4 ~

When Opportunity Knocks, Open the Door

One sound idea is all one needs to achieve success.
Success comes to those who become success conscious.
—Napoleon Hill

WHILE PARTICIPATING IN THE EDUCATION WITH INDUSTRY (EWI) Program in Atlanta, I continued working on my master's degree in business management, and successfully finished all of my course requirements. Obtaining my master's degree was very important to me and my family because it continued my assault on the educational legacy in our family. Poverty was taking a beating from me and I was glad to throw another punch for academic success and give my siblings hope and belief to do the same thing.

Two of my brothers followed my lead and earned their master's degrees. My siblings are young, and I believe they will continue to achieve academic excellence because we need to continue aspiring for success.

In June 1985, I successfully completed the EWI program in Financial Management at National Data Corporation (NDC). The Air Force Institute of Technology forwarded my program completion certificate to NDC managers and they took me to lunch at the Ritz Carlton in the Buckhead section of Atlanta. I said my goodbyes to my supervisor and friends, packed my bags for my new assignment, and drove to Scott Air Force Base in Belleville, Illinois.

I enjoyed living in Atlanta because it was an up and coming city in 1985. When I departed Atlanta, I had a few tears in my eyes because I knew I would miss my family and friends that lived there. I would return years later for the 1996 Olympic Games and have a wonderful time.

I am not complaining about the location of some of my Air Force assignments; however, I joined the Air Force to see the world. The Air Force determined that the world for me was going to be in the Midwest section of the United States. St. Louis, Missouri is located twenty miles west of Belleville, Illinois. After I arrived in Belleville, I realized I had never seen so many cornfields in my entire life.

My sponsor was excellent, and when I arrived at Scott AFB it was a very lively base because it was home to Headquarters Air Mobility Command (AMC) and Headquarters Air Force Communications Command (AFCC). I was assigned to HQ AFCC Comptroller's office. My tour of duty began on June 30, 1985, as a cost analysis officer.

I was responsible for a $3.6 billion acquisition program called the Inter-Service Agency/Automated Message Processing Exchange (I-SA/AMPE) program.

I became director of the cost/schedule control systems criteria (C/SCSC) team which meant I lead a team of twelve people, including contractors, to conduct reviews on the prime contractor's progress of the I-SA/AMPE program.

My acquisition knowledge, persuasiveness, and diplomacy helped Major General Gerald Prather, AFCC's Commander. General Prather's leadership team relied on my analysis to determine the feasibility of staying the course or terminating the multibillion dollar I-SA/AMPE contract.

Not only did I work for great leaders at HQ AFCC, I also worked for Lieutenant Colonel Don Hale, Director of Cost at

AFCC. I was given responsibilities in the area of subsequent application reviews (SARs), which meant I worked in the Los Angeles area on a frequent basis. I also worked in Burlington, North Carolina with the subcontractor, so in retrospect I had a great assignment at Scott AFB and continued to learn and progress as a junior officer.

I met outstanding senior level African-American officers who went out of their way to help junior officers like myself by mentoring us. Senior officer mentoring cut down my learning curve faster than I could have done on my own. Colonel John Culver sticks out as one of the most influential officers I have ever met. He had tremendous officership and leadership abilities that made me sit up and listen to him when he spoke. I also admired Colonel Culver's wife, who was a tremendous officer and leader in her own right, and had tremendous influence on the young women officers. There is no way I can forget the outstanding people I met at Scott AFB.

During my tour I worked with a brilliant young officer by the name of Lieutenant Latisha Dotson. Had Latisha not separated from the Air Force, she would likely have been promoted to the rank of colonel. I know talented people when I meet them, and Latisha was one of those talented young officers. Another individual I met and truly admired was Richard Hall; he was a pilot and an Air Force Academy graduate. Latisha and Richard got married and they make a great couple; I wish them the best life has to offer.

One of my best friends is a man by the name of Chris Brown, an Air Force Academy graduate. Chris was assigned to AMC in the communications field during his assignment at Scott. Chris had aspirations to make the Olympic wrestling team and when I met him it was always in the gym. I was playing basketball, perfecting my game for the base team and championships.

Chris was perfecting his wrestling skills and competed for the Olympics, but fell short. Chris retired after fifteen years of military service, then moved to San Diego to be with the future Mrs. Claudia Brown. They also have three beautiful children.

Abe Morrall is another individual who brought a lot of positive energy to the officer corps at Scott. We were a part of a group called the Air Force Company Grade Officer Mentoring Action Program (AFCOMAP) for officers.

AFCOMAP was and is an effective mentoring program that provides leadership, knowledge, and networking for new arriving officers and those currently assigned on base. It took the guesswork out of finding out how the base operates, because senior officers keep junior officers on a positive and progressive path of becoming better officers.

I have prayed many a night for AFCOMAP and its members because it was a blessing for me and other officers to have a place to go to discuss the problems we encountered. Just having someone listen is therapeutic, and AFCOMAP provided an outlet for me. An individual who continues to carry the torch for AFCOMAP is Colonel Ken McKinney; he is still doing a great job with our young Air Force officers.

Attending the base chapel at Scott AFB each Sunday was important to me. In fact, if it were not for my spiritual life, which included praise and worship, I would not be the person I am today. I am not perfect, as none of us are, but I believe when we have an opportunity to improve our spiritual, physical, and mental lives we are in essence helping make the world a better place to live. I was thankful to God for allowing me the opportunity to have a place to worship.

In 1986 HQ AFCC offered officers an opportunity to compete for their speaker's bureau. Individuals selected to represent AFCC became known as command briefers. I attended a couple of Toastmaster Club meetings at Scott AFB; however, I did not join because my schedule did not afford me a lot of extra time.

Practice sessions for command briefing selections were conducted in the command headquarters staff office. I never get nervous when speaking because I have done it my entire life. I routinely don't feel pressure or get nervous when I am speaking, so I breezed through the practice sessions and thought I had done well. One of the airmen sitting in on the practice session looked at me strangely, and I could tell he was not impressed with my performance.

Mind you, I always save my best for the platform and actual performance, so I knew I would do well with an audience no matter what the size. Needless to say, I was selected to tour the various universities throughout the U.S. in an effort to recruit AFROTC cadets for assignment to HQ AFCC.

My first trip with the not-so-convinced airman was to the New England states. This was going to be a fun trip because my former roommate Cliff Frye was stationed at Hanscom Field. I would have an opportunity to visit with him and his family while in the Boston area.

Prior to departing, the airman and I signed for and secured the customized minivan we were to drive to the New England states. We left Belleville, Illinois en route to Massachusetts, Connecticut, New Hampshire, and Vermont.

We used the buddy system while driving to the New England states. Thankfully, we had a great music selection because we were traveling in the hinterlands for some periods of the trip. We only stopped for gas or the restroom, and were fortunate to have a van with two gas tanks. As you know, gas was not as expensive as it is today. After driving across the state of Pennsylvania, the airman and I felt as though we had discovered America because it seemed to take forever.

The airman traveled with me because he operated the nine-projector slide presentation. Sounds antiquated by today's standards, doesn't it? My job consisted of providing a nine-projector synchronized slide presentation and speech; I also had a stage length screen behind me. I had to be on cue when the jet aircraft appeared on the screen; otherwise, the audience would know I was either ahead or behind during my speech. No pressure.

First stop on our speaking tour was St. Michael's College in Vermont, and it was very successful. After the presentation, the airman and I decided to visit some of the local entertainment spots and it gave us an opportunity to review and discuss my speech. The airman told me he thought my command briefing rehearsal stank. I laughed at his comment and then informed him that I always save my best performance for my audience.

Then he shocked me by stating, "I have traveled with a lot of command briefers prior to this trip, and you are the best speaker I have ever heard or worked with." He went on to state that my speaking performance at St Michael's College was perfect. I laughed at him again and said, you are kidding me, and he said you deliver your speech differently when you are in front of an audience. I told him that I take a lot of pride in what I do and I would not have accepted the responsibility to represent HQ AFCC as a command briefer if I didn't think I could deliver for them on the platform. He thanked me for being a professional.

The airman and I continued on the New England tour. I spoke at Norwich University, Boston University, and the University of Connecticut. The University of Connecticut is located in Storrs, Connecticut, which afforded me the opportunity to see one of my good friends, Darrel Moody. Darrel and I had been stationed at Wright-Patterson AFB together. He separated from the Air Force and was employed in Connecticut during the time frame I was on my speaking engagement in the New England states.

In retrospect, being a command briefer at Scott AFB played a major role in my decision to become a motivational speaker; however, I will discuss this later in the book. The bottom line is that I truly enjoyed being on the speaking circuit in support of HQ AFCC.

What time is it? It's time for more leadership training. Air

Force officers as well as enlisted personnel must attend leadership training courses throughout their military career. Leadership is the most important discipline for military personnel, regardless of the branch of service, and is a way of life in the military.

In 1986, I enrolled in my first-level leadership program, which is Squadron Officer School (SOS). I decided to complete the program through correspondence, which was a great way to do it because one could remain at their duty station and still receive credit for completion. I completed SOS in May, 1987.

In July 1986, I departed Scott AFB to attend the Comptroller Staff Officer Course (CSOC) at Sheppard AFB in Wichita Falls, Texas. CSOC is an advanced comptroller program for officers projected to progress into the field grade ranks—the level after company grade officer rank. I graduated from CSOC in August, 1986.

I met some very nice officers at CSOC and one in particular was a fellow by the name of Leathon Magee; he was called Buck. Buck was from a wonderful family in Mississippi and had family members in Texas as well. Buck took me to his sister's house in the Dallas, Fort Worth area which was two hours south of Wichita Falls, Texas.

Prior to attending Wichita Falls, I had never visited Texas before. After visiting the Dallas area, it seemed like a nice place to live. Little did I know I would be living in Texas less than a year later.

I was prepared to return to Scott AFB to get back to the comptroller business. Just after returning, a slot for Squadron Officer School (SOS) in residence opened up at Maxwell AFB in Montgomery, Alabama. I began processing my paperwork for the SOS in residence program which was a nine-week program.

It was great being a member of SOS Class 87E, Section E-53 for those officers who remember the long hot summer in Montgomery, Alabama. The program consisted of military history, war gaming, leadership exercises, athletic competitions, and academics. My section, good old Section E, received the academic achievement award for the highest academic performance in the squadron. Our section also won the competitive leadership excellence award for the highest section athletic performance in Squadron E, Class 87-E.

I flew back to Scott AFB after SOS and settled into my duties. It seemed as though I had been gone for a year. I worked for a brilliant officer by the name of Colonel James Daugherty who was the AFCC Comptroller and was as sharp as any officer I had ever met. I enjoyed working in his directorate and I was doing my best to make his job easier.

In late 1987, I received a call from my friend Darrel Moody. I had visited Darrell in Connecticut while on the speaking tour. I was aware he had left the Air Force after five or so years, and knew he had a good corporate job. He passed on the name of his headhunter, or corporate recruiter, to me and I retained it.

Prior to 1987, I had never given consideration to separating from the Air Force. However, I began to think about what life would be like after the military. I flew to North Carolina for the Christmas holidays and discussed it with my parents, and they didn't understand why I was considering leaving the Air Force. My spirit was telling me to give the corporate world a try, and thus began the knock on the door. I still had not finalized my decision to separate, and had not discussed it with my leadership at Scott AFB.

Happy New Year! 1988 was going to be a great year for me, and my life was definitely going to change. I continued to flirt with the idea of separating from the Air Force and decided to give the corporate recruiter a call. After speaking with him, I arranged to meet him in Fort Knox, Kentucky, so he could review my personnel records and I could see if I wanted him to represent me.

The orientation meeting went well, and I didn't have anything to lose as far as meeting with him. After leaving the meeting, I knew I would be leaving the Air Force. I knew I could land a job with one of the Fortune 500 companies, and this could help my family and me financially.

After returning to Scott AFB, I met with Colonel Daugherty and informed him of my plans to separate from the Air Force, and then I discussed it with my co-workers. No one could believe I was going to leave the Air Force. They were stunned, but I wasn't.

In March 1988, I flew to Charlotte, North Carolina, to prepare for my interviews with Fortune 500 companies. After two days of intense preparation consisting of interviewing skills, resume writing and professional business etiquette, I was ready for my interviews.

The way the process worked for the headhunter and Fortune 500 companies was for junior officers to list the companies they prospectively wanted to work for. After the initial listings were reviewed, the profiles were screened to see if a fit existed for a particular job that needed to be filled by an employer.

Once the companies reviewed the personnel in the good fit pool, the headhunter would inform the prospective interviewee to review the company background provided to them.

Mobil Chemical Company and Michelin Tire Company requested me to interview with them. Both interviews went well, and my speaking abilities really helped out because you have to really understand how a company operates before you can interview successfully.

After completing the initial interviews, I flew to Mobil Chemical Company in Beaumont, Texas. The interview with Mobil went well and I felt they wanted me to work for them. Even though I didn't know a lot about the petrochemical industry, the name and reputation of Mobil was quite convincing for me to give them the edge as far as long-term employment was concerned.

A week later, I flew to Michelin Tire Company in Greenville, South Carolina. The interview at Michelin was just as good; however, I had already lived in North Carolina for twenty-one years. Location played a factor in my decision to decline Michelin's offer. I received an offer from both Mobil and Michelin; however, I wanted to live in the state of Texas, so Mobil was the best choice for me.

I flew back to Scott AFB and announced my decision to my leadership team and separated from the Air Force on May 31, 1988. I had a luncheon with my family members and friends, and we were crying because everyone knew how much I loved the Air Force and the wonderful people at Scott AFB.

Many of my friends asked me if I regret separating from the Air Force, and that's a fair question. I want to let you in on a little secret of mine. Remember I revealed the fact that one of the gifts God gave me was that of a dreamer. I had dreamt of working at Mobil a couple of years before I had ever visited Texas. By the same token, I knew I could join the Air Force Reserves or the Air National Guard so I would stay connected to the Air Force and my friends.

The movers packed my household goods and transported them to Beaumont, Texas. I was a civilian again and I was going to take advantage of my new role as a financial manager with Mobil Chemical Company, and I did. When opportunity knocked, I opened the door.

ACTION PLAN #1

We All Have Greatness on the Inside of Us

ALL OF US WERE BORN WITH GREATNESS ON THE INSIDE OF US and I can prove it to you. We have greatness on the inside of us whenever we inspire and motivate other people. Other people consist of our families, soldiers, airmen, sailors, active duty, Marines, Guard and Reserve and Coast Guard personnel. We have greatness on the inside of us if we make a positive difference in the lives of others and our nation. We have greatness on the inside of us if we love our country and are willing to lay down our lives for it.

Everything we need to be successful is at hand. We need to look no further than the books we read at home or in the unit or squadron where we perform our duties. Year after year we continue to make progress in our lives. From birth we were given gifts, talents, and a will to determine exactly what we want to be in life. We should continually read books, go to the movies, and be around positive people so they can inspire us to discover the greatness we have on the inside of us.

Please write down seven things that let you know you have greatness on the inside of you.

1. _____

2. _____

3. _____

4. _____

5. _____

6. _____

7. _____

ACTION PLAN #2

In Order to Soar like an Eagle, We Must Fly Above the Clouds

TO HELP THEM SOAR, EAGLES USE THERMALS, WHICH ARE RISING currents of warm air and updrafts generated by terrain, such as valley edges or mountain slopes. Soaring is accomplished with very little wing-flapping, which enables eagles to conserve energy. Long-distance migration flights are accomplished by climbing high in a thermal, and then gliding downward to catch the next thermal, where the process is repeated.

We use the same principles as the eagle; we use momentum to ride the wave until our mission is completed. We use the network we built, which is generated by our professional relationships and connections. Success is accomplished with very little effort after we discover the importance of being professional military personnel; we don't have to expend as much energy getting to the top if we are willing to put aside our personal goals for the success of our squadron or unit. Long distances are not an issue if we use technology such as video teleconferences to cut down on migratory flights. The only thing the troops need is one another in order to make our battle plans become reality. We shall be victorious today, and soar like the eagles in the future.

Please list seven ways you can help improve your branch of the service and provide your inputs to your commander.

1. _____

2. _____

3. _____

4. _____

5. _____

6. _____

7. _____

Having an Eagle's Point of View

All eagles are renowned for their excellent eyesight. Eagles have two centers of focus; this allows them to see forward and to the side at the same time.

High-achieving military personnel are renowned for their vision; in fact, they are called visionary. You have the foresight to see things before they happen because you have developed a 360-degree perspective of what you believe your success will look like.

My vision for success looks like: _____

_____

_____

～ 5 ～

Diversity is Imperative
to the Bottom Line

Go after your dream with a sense of entitlement.
Know that you have the power to achieve it and that you deserve
it. Be willing to get up into life's face, grab it by the collar and say,
"Give it UP! It's my dream."

—Les Brown

I BEGAN WORKING FOR MOBIL CHEMICAL COMPANY IN MAY, 1988. Living in Texas was all I had imagined it would be and I enjoyed it. Even though it was quite a distance from North Carolina, I knew I could get a flight if one of my parents became ill. Little did I know how often I would be visiting my family in North Carolina.

Prior to separating from the Air Force, military personnel instructed me to sign up for the inactive reserves by June 1, 1988, just in case I wanted to join the Air Force Reserves to serve on a part-time basis. Gerald Reich, my supervisor at Mobil Chemical, was very generous and understanding. He took time out of his schedule to drive me to the 147th Fighter Wing, Texas Air National Guard located fifteen miles south of Houston at Ellington Field National Guard Base in Houston, Texas to be sworn in on the morning of June 1, 1988. I not only met the deadline but the decision would play a critical role in me returning to the Air Force two years later.

My supervisor served in the Army and was a member of the Army National Guard during the time of my employment. I was a financial analyst, and one of the reasons I was hired by Mobil was because they understood diversity, and aligned their diversity program to their strategic plan. They hired talented young minorities in order to transition from local hires to outside hires. In essence, Mobil was thinking global as opposed to national in their hiring.

In August 1988, I was almost thirty years old and decided to purchase my first house in Beaumont, Texas. I was the only African-American living in my neighborhood, and my neighbors were absolutely wonderful. Any time I threw a party I invited my neighbors, and they invited me to their social activities as well.

Mobil Chemical's Olefins and Aromatic Plant in Beaumont, Texas is located one hundred ten miles east of Houston, Texas and forty-five miles west of Lake Charles, Louisiana. It was a small town when I lived and worked there; however, it's growing relatively fast nowadays.

I still have a picture taken of me on my first day on the job. I guess I was excited to be there because the picture looks as though my eyes were wide open. It didn't take long for me to snap out of the daze because I was tasked to work on major projects upon my arrival.

I was fortunate to work for a supervisor who had served in the Army and was a member of the Army National Guard, because he understood the dedication I brought to my job. My responsibilities consisted of analyzing monthly income reports and analyzing production and product sales for benzene and toluene. I was working at the Olefins and Aromatics Plant and I never knew how sensitive I was to the smell of chemicals until I walked outside the main plant building to my office in a trailer.

It was not unusual to see alligators near the wharf where we worked. One had to be paying attention; otherwise, things could get ugly very quickly. The only time I worried about alligators was when we were conducting our audit at midnight. One had better have on a good pair of boots, along with a hard hat with a light on it.

I didn't regret separating from the Air Force in 1988 because I am happiest when I am able to live my dreams. From May 1988 to January 1990, I was happily employed by Mobil Chemical. I thoroughly enjoyed working with the people at the Olefins and Aromatics Plant as well as the district headquarters office located near the Houston Intercontinental Airport and our plant near the Port of Houston.

People truly make the difference in a work environment and Mobil Chemical was no exception. I participated in monthly meetings in the Houston District office as well as supporting audits. Mobil also had a polyethylene plant in Beaumont and I had friends who worked there as well.

I was fortunate to be in on the ground floor of a facility Mobil purchased in Chalmette, Louisiana, just north of New Orleans. The Chalmette Plant is located near the site of the Battle of New Orleans, which America won, forcing Britain to recognize the United States' claims to Louisiana.

Craig Mouton and his wife Pat and their family are friends of mine and I truly value their friendship. We stay in touch with each other on a frequent basis. Annette Byerly and her family are wonderful people and I love to visit their home because Annette's mother cooks great gumbo.

I received a call from my family in Henderson regarding my mother, who was having more pronounced health problems. My mother was scheduled for triple bypass heart surgery at Duke Medical Center, which is forty miles from Henderson. I flew to North Carolina for the surgery and prayed with my family for our mother's surgery to go well.

Duke Medical Center is a premier hospital, so we knew she was in good hands. The surgery was very successful. The staff at Duke informed my family and me that if my mother follows their guidance she could resume a normal lifestyle without much pain or abnormalities.

After returning to Beaumont, Texas, I discussed my mother's condition with my supervisor and management. I also informed my supervisor that I was seeking a transfer to the East Coast so I could be closer to my parents in case something else happened. Unfortunately, they were not able to accommodate my request, so I began seeking employment in North Carolina as well as the Mid-Atlantic region of the United States.

I knew it would likely take more time to find suitable employment on the East Coast, so in the meantime I hunkered down until an opportunity presented itself. I applaud Mobil Oil Company for having the vision to press forward to the mark by scheduling diversity awareness training for its personnel. In 1988, I was offered an opportunity to attend Mobil's first annual diversity awareness training in McLean, Virginia.

I flew from Houston to McLean, just outside of Washington, DC, with roughly twenty other personnel from various Mobil Oil Product Divisions. We were all African-American men and women. The diversity session was led by a husband and wife team, and it was designed to help us understand the direction Mobil was moving from a strategic perspective. In my opinion, Mobil was on the cutting edge of diversity, and I was fortunate to be a part of it.

After completing the first half of the diversity session sponsored by Mobil, I returned to Beaumont, Texas. A few months later, I returned to McLean to complete the second half of the program. Little did I know at the time how instrumental the diversity sessions would be on my life.

Mobil Oil Company was proactive and a forerunner in understanding the advantage of hiring a diverse workforce. I believe senior leadership at Mobil researched the projected demographics and took the initiative to position themselves to capitalize on the talent available to them. I can personally say

Mobil invested in hiring me, and I will be forever grateful to them because they didn't have to hire me.

A couple of months after the first diversity training session, I returned to McLean, and I began to sense a difference in my spirit, that a change was about to take place. Earlier in the year, I was offered an Air Force Reserve position that was opening at Tinker AFB in Oklahoma City, Oklahoma; however, it fell through. My military personnel records, along with my request for a Reserve slot, were still in the Air Force Reserve personnel system.

I successfully completed Mobil Oil's first-of-its-kind diversity training program. I took a taxi to Washington National Airport. The plane took off and we flew over the Washington Monument to capture great views of our nation's capitol. All of a sudden my inner voice said, "you are going to be coming back to Washington to live." It was one of those moments in time that makes you laugh as if to say, "right."

The irony of the event that occurred on my departure flight back to Beaumont was followed up by a dream I had a few days later. In the dream, I remember seeing myself in an Air Force uniform, and my supervisor came to my desk to talk with me about the budget. My dream was one of the most surreal I have ever had.

In September 1989, I was working on the monthly activity report. My supervisor informed me I had a phone call. I answered the phone and a Lieutenant Colonel Craig Shelton was on the other end of the line. He said, "Paul, I reviewed your personnel records located at Peterson AFB, Colorado, and I understand you applied for a Reserve slot in the comptroller career field." I responded by saying, "You are correct, sir."

Lieutenant Colonel Shelton informed me he was an Active Guard Reservist (AGR) with the Air National Guard located in the Pentagon. Colonel Shelton went on to state he was interested in knowing whether I wanted to return to active duty, because he was forming a cost analysis shop for the Air National Guard (ANG), and he was interested in having me work for him.

First of all, I was breathless. I told Colonel Shelton that I would give it consideration and that I'd call him back in a couple of days.

After speaking with my parents about the opportunity, they said, "You know you love the Air Force. Why not go back in if they want you to return to duty?" I contacted Colonel Shelton as I had promised, and we talked for a few minutes. Then I asked him where I would be stationed, and he said in the Pentagon with him. I am sure he thought I had fainted because I was stunned. This decision helped me get back to the East Coast so I could be closer to my parents and siblings and return to the Air Force.

A couple of things had to happen prior to me returning to duty, and one was to pass a physical exam. I had been eating a lot of Cajun food while in Texas, and had gained over thirty pounds because I worked, slept, worked and slept—after all, the corporate world is demanding.

I only had three weeks to come within Air Force weight standards prior to the physical exam at Randolph AFB in San Antonio, Texas. I had to come up with a winning formula for taking my weight down to Air Force standards. Do you believe I could lose thirty pounds in three weeks? You had better place your trust in a winner because I was a winner.

I lost thirty-three pounds in three weeks by praying seven times a day, cutting out all fast and junk foods including condiments. The first day after work I walked to the high school down the street from my house and ran a mile, then stretched for an hour. The next morning I attended an aerobics class. That evening I ran two miles around the track. The third day, I lifted weights in the morning. After work, I ran three miles around the track.

Things were looking good for me and I was beginning to get the hang of things now. I attended an aerobics class before work, and then after work I ran four miles around the track. I ran around the track because I could monitor my mileage and gauge my progress.

I was getting the impurities out of my body, and the weight started to come off, and I was becoming very svelte again. Two days before the weigh-in I was three pounds over the limit, so I decided to take my last long run before the physical exam. I ran ten miles around the track, and then headed straight for the hot and cold sauna bath and drank lots of water. The evening before the physical exam, I went to the River Walk and had a light dinner and drank lots of fluids.

When I awakened the next morning I was two pounds above my limit, so I ran two miles, rode the stationary bike and treadmill, and hit the sauna. I was two pounds under the standard and then I immediately went to weigh in and nearly fainted. Then I requested water and the blood work began.

A few weeks later all of the blood work and physical exam paperwork was completed and the doctor asked me one important question: "Have you recently lost a lot of weight?" I answered yes, and he said my blood work indicated I had lost significant weight and what I had done was very dangerous.

I understood what the doctor was saying and then I informed him that my desire to return to the Air Force was worth losing thirty-three pounds in three weeks. The doctor looked at me as if I had lost my mind, but I was very serious, because losing the weight was not as significant as me having an opportunity to be close to my parents and siblings in North Carolina.

Sure, losing thirty-three pounds was not a wise thing to do. The problem was gaining that much weight in the first place. The only other thing the doctor said was, "Good luck in your new military career," and I told him, "Thank you."

After completing my security background check, I was cleared to return to the Air Force and awaited my orders from San Antonio. Unfortunately, someone at the Air Force assignments office didn't process my orders as initially agreed.

I met with my supervisor at Mobil and informed him of my plans. I submitted my resignation letter and was scheduled to depart the week of Christmas, 1989. I had a small party with my dear friends, hired a property management company to lease my house, and put my household goods in storage.

I packed as many of my essentials as I could in the car and drove to North Carolina to prepare for my new assignment in the Pentagon. I enjoyed a wonderful Christmas in Henderson with my parents and siblings, and then drove to Maryland to await my orders.

My cousin Cheryl and her husband Steve moved from Atlanta to Greenbelt, Maryland, they invited me to spend New Year's Eve with them. I drove from North Carolina to Maryland on December 31st and welcomed in the New Year. Happy New Year, America! You are beautiful and this is going to be my decade! And it was.

It was a blessing from God for me to be able to reach Claude Jones, my classmate from Shaw University. The last time I saw Claude was in 1987 when he was on temporary duty at Scott AFB. Claude had since separated from the Air Force and was working in the Washington, DC, area.

Claude and his wife Linda graciously allowed me to stay at their home until my orders arrived. Two months later, Claude and Linda informed me they were expecting their second child. I moved into an apartment so they could prepare for the new addition to their family. I will always be grateful for their hospitality and love because they helped me at a time when I didn't have anywhere else to turn for help.

ACTION PLAN #1

Valuing Diversity

AT ONE TIME OR ANOTHER, WE HAVE EITHER HEARD OR SEEN news reports discussing the influx of immigrants from other countries risking life and limb to get to America. The people trying to get to America understand that if they can reach our shores, they will have a chance at unlimited opportunities and a better quality of life. The United States of America offers an opportunity for many immigrants to serve our country, while ensuring them citizenship and chance to live a life with liberty, freedom, and hope. America is one of the most diverse countries in the world, and we will continue to see her demographics change.

With our changing demographics, we all need to understand the dynamics taking place in our military manpower. Please list seven reasons why the diversity of our military forces will give the United States a battlefield advantage in the future.

1. _____

2. _____

3. _____

4. _____

5. _____

6. _____

7. _____

Diversity is playing a key role in the way our military is managed today, and leadership is answering the call to duty. Our top military leaders must ensure that diversity is a part of its strategic plan; otherwise, our military will experience troop shortages. Results reflect that inclusion of diverse personnel is more conducive to better ideas, better work environments, and higher levels of productivity.

It's important to understand that in order to maintain troop strength levels, we need personnel who can speak the language of the countries we go to war with. Diversity is about other points of view contributing to mission success.

ACTION PLAN #2

To Understand Diversity is to Understand One's Self

IN 1988, WHILE EMPLOYED BY MOBIL CHEMICAL COMPANY IN Texas, I was selected by corporate leadership to attend a first-of-its kind diversity training program. I had never heard about diversity training programs prior to working for Mobil, but I looked forward to learning about it. I discovered a lot about diversity as a body of work, but most importantly, I learned more about myself. Unless I understood myself, it would be difficult to understand and appreciate others in my work environment. Diversity is about understanding our similarities and differences, and it will serve us well in the future.

Webster's Dictionary defines the word diversity as different. We can all agree that as individuals, none of us are the same. The magic of diversity is that once we understand ourselves, our likes, dislikes, biases and tolerances, we can more easily embrace others.

The key to understanding diversity is to understand one's self and to treat other people with respect and dignity. I have never forgotten the lessons I learned from my diversity training in 1988, I have since attended diversity-train-the-trainer programs and again I learned even more about myself.

Please list seven contributions you can make to diversity in your branch of service. Discuss them with your human resource representative, your diversity manager, or your commander. Your contributions to diversity will make a world of difference to our military.

1. _____

2. _____

3. _____

4. _____

5. _____

6. _____

7. _____

Diversity programs will continue to play a significant role in the military. Valuing diversity is the key to improving our military bottom line, which is fighting and winning against enemies foreign and domestic.

~ 6 ~

Elevating Our
Levels of Excellence

First, we cannot overload the human brain.
This divinely created brain has fourteen billion cells.
If used to the maximum, this human computer inside our heads
could contain all the knowledge of humanity
from the beginning of the world to the present
and still have room left over.

—Dr. Ben Carson

In January 1990, I contacted the personnel officer at Randolph AFB regarding my military orders. They informed me that the orders were forthcoming; however, it would take over five months before they arrived.

The only recourse for me at the time was to apply for a job. I applied for and was hired by GTE Mobile Communications in Alexandria, Virginia, and I became a salesman. I sold cellular phones for five months and interviewed for other jobs in the Washington area until my orders to return to extended active duty (EAD) arrived.

The first week after New Year's I met an individual at a job fair in Maryland. He asked me if there was anything he could do to help me since I was new to the Washington, DC, area. I asked him if he could recommend a church I could attend.

The gentleman requested me to follow him to church on Sunday and I did. A few months later, I became a member of

From the Heart Church Ministries located in Temple Hills, Maryland. I rededicated my life to God and was a member of From the Heart for over thirteen years.

When I initially joined From the Heart, it was an African Methodist Episcopal Zion church. Prior to leaving, it's denominational structure was changed to Nondenominational. I truly enjoyed the word of God that resonated throughout the congregation.

After becoming a member of From the Heart I met Jonathan, and he and I became good friends. Jonathan was a lawyer and had a lot of connections with the Washington, DC, area's professional sports athletes. I was able to sustain myself financially by selling cell phones and activation services to a number of the athletes. I was also able to integrate myself into the Washington scene by attending events with the athletes; for example, I attended the Washington Redskins football minicamps.

I'll never forget meeting Jack Kent Cooke, owner of the Redskins, and his wife at a minicamp. Joe Gibbs was the coach of the Redskins. The Washington Redskins had a great team and nothing could compare to attending a football game at RFK Stadium.

I became friends with a number of the Redskin football players, especially those from North Carolina. On a few occasions, I would hang out with a few of my Kappa Alpha Psi fraternity brothers, who played on the team.

I also met and socialized with some of the Washington Bullets basketball players and attended different events with them. Even though I was waiting for my military orders, I was really enjoying myself and getting to find my identity in the Washington, DC, area.

My former college classmate, Claude Jones and his wife Linda introduced me to her sister, who worked for the Environmental Protective Agency (EPA), and they arranged an interview for me. I went to the interview at the EPA, and was projected to be hired as a budget analyst at the GS-14 grade. I was going to accept the job because it looked very appealing and the salary was very good.

A week later, I received a call from Lieutenant Colonel Shelton regarding my orders. Two weeks later, I received a call from Randolph AFB and they informed me that my orders had been disseminated and that I was to report to the Pentagon on June 14, 1990.

I reported to EAD, in-processed, and was back in my Air Force uniform. Earlier I mentioned I had a dream about being back in the Air Force sitting at my desk in an office. After walking into Lieutenant Colonel Shelton's office, he directed me to my desk. I sat in my chair at the desk and it was like déjà vu all over again. I dreamt I was sitting at my desk and less than a year later I was living my dream.

Colonel Shelton introduced me to all of the staff at the Air National Guard (ANG) and I was assigned to the Cost Analysis Branch. 1990 was the first time the ANG Headquarters set up a cost analysis shop, and I was going to play a key role in the transformation.

I was selected for return to EAD by the Voluntary Reserve Officer Recall Board, and it was obvious to me that this doesn't happen very often. The recall process is very competitive; thus, I was not going to take anything for granted. There were no guarantees for the next higher grade for promotion or continuation of duty beyond two years.

The only thing on my mind was elevating my level of excellence. I needed to remain relevant to the Air Force, and working in support of ANG programs and projects would help me accomplish my professional goals. I also knew that God was orchestrating my life; my dreams had already revealed to me that I would continue to progress in rank and responsibility. I had more than the faith of a mustard seed, so I knew I was going to excel while working for the ANG Comptroller Directorate.

Little did I know, Operation Desert Shield/Desert Storm was on the horizon. All of a sudden we were in a wartime situation in the Pentagon. I remember meeting General Colin Powell in the Pentagon. I shook General Powell's hand and exchanged pleasantries with him, and his mere presence motivated me to elevate my level of excellence.

After meeting General Colin Powell, I went back to my office and called my parents to tell them who I had met. They were laughing at me because they knew I was excited. It's a meeting I will never forget because General Powell was an African-American leader and represented the best of America.

The reason I stress the importance of seeing an African-American in a high-level leadership position is because it was not something I saw growing up in my community. I take a lot of pride in seeing General Powell accomplish and achieve so much—it meant officers such as me could achieve success in the military as well.

Of all the men I know, my father is at the head of the class in terms of leadership skills, because he set the tone by raising me from a boy to a man. I have never idolized any man; however, I hold people like Dr. King, Mr. Mandela, and General Powell in high esteem because of their unique journeys in life.

One of my initial projects was performing cost estimates for a foreign military sales program between the ANG and the Dutch government. Colonel Shelton and I worked long hours in the night preparing for negotiations with Dutch representatives in their Embassy, and came away with a memorandum of agreement between our two countries. We train Dutch students to become pilots. This is an excellent program, and it's one of several we have with various countries.

The reason I knew I was doing exactly what I was born to do while assigned to the Pentagon was because I was given great opportunities to elevate my level of excellence. For example, my office approved of me attending Total Quality Management

(TQM) Courses-in the early 1990s, military services were transitioning to TQM.

In February 1991, I was fortunate to attend The Philadelphia Area Council for Excellence (PACE) Transformation for Management of Quality and Productivity course presented by none other than Dr. W. Edwards Deming himself. I became the TQM guru for my office, and the tutelage of Dr. Deming helped me to become more productive.

Deep down on the inside of me, I understood my recall to active duty was not a guarantee that I would remain on duty beyond the two years I was initially assigned. I had promised myself that I would take care of the things in my control, and things not in my control would work themselves out just perfectly, and they did.

After returning to EAD, I decided to earn another master's degree. I wanted to give myself the best opportunity to remain on duty. I enrolled in and attended a satellite, masters degree program at Andrews AFB. I attended Florida Institute of Technology to obtain a degree in contract and acquisition management. The Air Force only provided tuition assistance if an officer signed up for a degree on their shortfall list, and my degree aspirations happened to fit their criteria.

I earned and received my second master's degree from Florida Institute of Technology in 1992.

I invited my entire office to the graduation ceremony and we had a great time. I had elevated my level of excellence once again. Each time I earned another degree, I always remembered just how hard it was for our family growing up in poverty. I was motivated to separate myself from the hurdles in life. When I accepted my second master's degree, it was for my mother and father and eight siblings, and it was yet another victory over our enemy—which was poverty.

The year 1992 resulted in a physical setback for me. It occurred one morning in the Pentagon Officer Athletic Center (POAC).

I was participating in a step aerobics class and twenty minutes into the routine, I began to see spots of all shapes and colors, and I didn't know what caused it. The staff in the gym thought I was having a heart attack, but I knew that wasn't the case.

In addition to the visual irregularities, I also was not able to speak properly. I would respond to the medics, but my words did not come out the way I stated them. In many ways, it was as if I was having an out-of-body experience and there was nothing I could do about it. I went to the doctor, but they couldn't identify the problem.

It took over four months for the doctors to localize my physical ailment, and it seemed as if my world were spinning upside down. I began to experience memory loss—In the morning, I would drive my car to work at the Pentagon, and at the end of the work day I could not remember where I parked my vehicle.

Two months after the crisis began, I slept an average of thirteen hours a night and felt as if I had only slept for an hour. I began to have an irregular heartbeat as well. My initial medical visits to Malcolm Grow Medical Center at Andrews Air Force Base with a neurologist proved fruitless.

I scheduled appointments with Walter Reed Army Medical Center because they had better facilities. For several months, I was under the diagnosis of a young Captain who specialized in neurology, and she never gave up on me. The Captain called me in for a final round of blood tests and after the results returned from the laboratory, I was diagnosed with Lymes Disease; I had been bitten by a deer tick.

I visited my younger brother John, an Army officer assigned to duty in Germany. Germany had a high incidence of Lymes Disease. I lived in Maryland, which had a lot of vegetation—an environment that is also conducive for my disorder. My doctor placed me in an inpatient status at Walter Reed Army Medical Center. I became an in-patient and received a spinal tap to check whether the Lymes titer had penetrated my brain. They checked the fluid; however, it had not gotten into my brain.

I received antibiotics for a couple of days and was given medication to get me back on my feet. It took me a year to fully recover. I recall a Capitol Hill staffer had Lymes Disease, but it wasn't detected in the early stages, and she will be paralyzed for the rest of her life.

Thank God for directing me to a doctor who never gave up on me—it was truly a blessing. I am forever thankful for my doctor, because she could have just given up on me, but she didn't.

Just after my bout with Lymes Disease, my supervisor notified me that the Air Force was going to release (accessions) personnel such as myself, because Operation Desert Storm was coming to an end. I was going to be released from duty; however, I now had ten years of duty on record. Unless I was brought back on duty, I was about to return to private industry again.

After discussing my options with my supervisor, I was scheduled to meet with Major General Philip Killey, Director of the Air National Guard (ANG). I truly admired General Killey and his wife—they are two super people. I had a lot of respect for him, not only as an officer, but as a man. General Killey asked me what I planned on doing after being released from duty for the second time. I stated that I would likely apply for a civil service job, or if an opportunity opened up in the Air National Guard I would take it.

Major General Killey said, "Paul, if you are interested in joining the Air National Guard I can help you." Without another word, General Killey called the comptroller in the office and said make it happen and that's how I became a member of the Air National Guard. I thanked General Killey and felt beholden to him. There was no way I could pay him back for this wonderful opportunity he had given me, except to help make his job easier through my work.

I will always hold Major General Killey in high esteem. He

is responsible for me writing this book because without his leadership, I would not be able to tell this story. Thank you, General and Mrs. Killey—may God continue to truly bless you and your family.

Because I controlled the things I could control, it helped me pave the way for yet another tour of duty in the Pentagon with the Air National Guard. Only this time I was an active guard reservist (AGR), title ten full-time officer. I became a member of the 145th AW located in Charlotte, North Carolina, with my duty assignment in the Pentagon.

I would be remiss if I didn't acknowledge the leadership at the 145th Airlift Wing (AW) in Charlotte. Without the leadership, vision, and support of my North Carolina Air Guard brethren, the likelihood is that I would not have retired. Major General Gerald Rudisill, The Adjutant General (TAG) of North Carolina was also an absolute joy to work with and without his support over the years I would not have realized my dreams in the military.

In January 1994, I received a call from the ANG personnel section, and they asked me if I was sitting down. The airman on the other end of the line informed me that I would be promoted to the rank of Major in the Air National Guard. It was a good thing I was sitting, because I would likely have fainted otherwise. I was on cloud nine and could not believe it.

Major General Donald Shepperd, Director of the Air National Guard, hosted my promotion ceremony in the Pentagon. My parents never attended any of my promotions because their health was on a steady decline; however, my Uncle John and Aunt Virginia from Mount Vernon, New York, represented me at my promotion ceremony.

No one could top Gen. Shepperd when it came to promoting someone—he knew how to put the icing on the cake. He is a very inspirational officer and highly respected throughout the world. People like General Shepperd will never know how much they are appreciated. He has made a tremendous difference in the lives of others with his leadership and support. I am blessed to know him.

General Sheppard held my Air Force jacket and he humorously stated, "It's not everyday a General Officer holds your jacket for you." My Uncle John and a friend of mine pinned the Major's rank on my uniform. I am now a Major in the Air National Guard and I have become a field grade officer—who knew?

ACTION PLAN #1

Determination is Imperative to Your Success

IT DOES NOT MATTER WHERE YOU COME FROM OR WHAT SCHOOL you attended, determination is imperative to your success. If we were to tell our friends we have a goal of becoming the best soldier or airman we can be, they will give us ten reasons why we can't. We have completed our basic, intermediate, and advanced courses and we have what it takes to be the best, because we have invested in ourselves. Our determination in and of itself will provide the momentum we need to ride the wave to not only be the best airman or soldier, but to receive the medals to go along with the designation.

We all have a spirit on the inside of us, and with determination, we can do whatever our minds can conceive. Please list five things you are determined to achieve while in the military.

1. _____

2. _____

3. _____

4. _____

5. _____

Now that we have identified and written down the five things we are determined to achieve, we must be fully persuaded to do the work necessary to make our dreams a reality. Our ultimate goal is to succeed, and the way to ensure success is to be determined.

How can anyone tell us we can't accomplish our goals when they don't have our vision for success?

Many successful people were initially told they would not be able to achieve their goals. Henry Ford wanted his engineers to build a V-8 engine because he wanted to become more competitive in the automobile industry. Mr. Ford's team of engineers doubted the feasibility of developing V-8 engines because they believed it was impossible.

Henry Ford repeatedly told his engineers they would build the V-8 engines for his company, no matter how long it took. Realizing their jobs were on the line, Ford engineers designed and built V-8 engines just as Henry Ford requested. Mr. Henry Ford was determined to succeed, and he was not to be denied because he knew the impact it would have on the car industry. As long as we have the determination of people like Henry Ford, we will be successful.

ACTION PLAN #2

Being the Best

IN ORDER TO BE THE BEST IN OUR CAREER FIELD AND ULTIMATELY become experts, we must elevate our level of excellence. We elevate our level of excellence by doing the things others won't do. What are some of the things we must do? I will explain.

To be the best we must have clearly defined goals that are unwavering in the face of adversity—in other words, our goals must stand up to our own scrutiny. Many are called, few are chosen to serve our country. Make a lasting impression through your service.

We must be passionate about what we are doing because without passion we will likely not see our goals through to fruition. The lifeline of success runs through a pipeline filled with passion.

We must believe in ourselves; otherwise, we may be swayed by any wind of doctrine. Our vision is our vision. It is okay to take advice, but we must make the final decision to use it.

When we walk into a room with our uniform on, we must know we are the best. Let your confidence stand on its own merit.

Never give up on achieving your goals and living your dreams, and always remember that failures are a permitted response and we can overcome them.

Please list seven ways you can elevate your level of excellence while serving your country. I encourage you to review them and put them into action.

1. _____

2. _____

3. _____

4. _____

5. _____

6. _____

7. _____

The difference between success and failure is our level of excellence. Strive for perfection while achieving your goals in the military.

*"When all else fails, rely on excellence;
it's the choice of champions."*
—Paul Lawrence Vann

$\sim$ 7 $\sim$

Motivation is the Key
to Our Success

Success is the progressive realization of a worthy idea.

—Earl Nightingale

DID I RECEIVE A BLESSING FROM ABOVE AFTER RECEIVING
Major General Killey's support for me joining the Air National
Guard (ANG)? Yes I did. After processing into the military
for the second time within three years, I was assigned to the
Directorate/Financial Management and Comptroller responsible to Director, Air National Guard (ANG) for Air Staff/
MAJCOM financial programming and management of ANG
financial resources. I helped establish policies and procedures
for ANG-appropriated funds. I also developed and justified
budget submissions to the Office of Secretary of Defense, the
Office of Management and Budget, and Congressional review
authorities.

As a financial staff officer, I was responsible for approximately $800 million in operations and maintenance (O&M)
budget requirements relating to ANG flying operations. I had
the fortune of working for a man by the name of Al Mahoney,
a brilliant man and an individual I hold in high esteem to this
day. Al was a green eyeshade type and was a very precise civilian budget analyst who knows the business inside and out. I
admired Al and learned a lot about the Pentagon budgeting

process from him. Our division chief was Lieutenant Colonel Tom Koch, who was an active duty Air Force officer working for the Air National Guard.

I was responsible for the Defense Business Operating Fund (DBOF) for the ANG. DBOF fulfills its role as a revolving fund by purchasing designated supplies from commercial sources, the Defense Logistics Agency, the General Services Administration, and the Departments of the Army and Air Force and then selling them. These supplies may be sold to a specific appropriation.

In 1994, I was reassigned within the budget directorate and was responsible for monitoring and evaluating legislation for three ANG appropriations totaling over $4 billion. This is when my military career really took off.

My duties consisted of developing Congressional presentations for the Chief of the National Guard Bureau and the Director of the Air National Guard, and editing the transcripts for their legislative testimony. I was also the focal point for the review of the Secretary of Defense, Program Budget Decisions (PBD) and Congressional inquiries on ANG budget issues.

My responsibilities and duties consisted of reviewing and summarizing Congressional committee reports and public laws for the Director of the Air National Guard and his staff. Little did I know this assignment would motivate and propel me to reach my next level of excellence.

A couple of months passed, and one day while sitting at my desk, I received a phone call from my mother's doctor, insisting that I hurry home because my mother was not going to make it. I immediately informed my supervisors, and they told me not to worry and to get home to look after my mother. I contacted my sisters at Wake Memorial Hospital, and I told them if they are asked to put our mother on life support, to do so.

It was time for me to drive the five hours from Washington, DC, to Raleigh, North Carolina. I stopped on the highway just to check on my mom's status. I asked my sister how my mom was doing, and she said not too good, so I hung up the phone and continued driving to Raleigh.

I prayed all the way to the hospital until I arrived and was immediately directed to her room. My entire family was there, except my father, who was unable to make it because of his health problems.

After arriving at Wake Memorial Hospital the doctor asked, "Paul, what do you want to do about your mother?" I said, "Didn't my sisters tell you that I said to put our mother on life support?" He said no. I said, "Proceed to put my mother on life support because every minute counts." The hospital staff was very accommodating, and they moved my mother into a hospital room. My family and I prayed together; then they headed back to Henderson, NC, which was forty-five miles north of Raleigh.

It was important for me to stay at my mom's bedside and I stayed for an entire month, helping the nurses take care of her and talking with the hospital chaplain. I contacted my supervisor and he told me to take care of my mother. This represented the highest honor I have ever received in my life. I was accorded an opportunity to look after my mother without having to worry about making it back to work; I needed the time to look inside myself and to listen to my inner voice once again.

Each day for thirty straight days, I went to the hospital chapel and was often the only person there, but I knew God was right there with me. Mother's Day was coming, so my family and I purchased flowers for our mother. My siblings were all happy that I had made the decision to put Mom on life support. Even though Mom was in a coma, we knew she could feel our presence in her room on her last earthly Mother's Day.

After a month sitting by my mother's bedside, I returned to work and thanked Lieutenant Colonel Tom Koch, my supervisor, and the rest of the staff for supporting my family during my mother's illness. My spirit told me to return home on

Saturday night and I did. I drove to Henderson to see my father and siblings, and then I told them I was heading to Raleigh to check on our mother.

I checked into the Residence Inn in Raleigh and contacted my brother who lived in Durham, and met him for dinner. I departed for the hospital at 9:00 pm. I arrived at the hospital, walked to my mother's hospital room, kissed her on the forehead, and prayed for a few minutes. Then I went to the chaplain's office to see if she was working that evening.

The chaplain was on duty that evening, and she walked with me back to my mother's hospital room. It was approaching midnight and the chaplain and I were sitting in the chairs next to my mom's bedside and we were talking about Jesus.

I explained that my mother was responsible for me being the person I am today because she taught me how to love unconditionally. My mother was my number one supporter in the entire world, and I owe my all to her for raising me the way she did.

It was approaching midnight and while the chaplain and I were talking, the nurse entered the room to check on my mother. She discovered that my mother had passed on; it was peaceful. The chaplain and nurse gave me time to grieve in my mother's hospital room, so I prayed that my mother was going to be with the Lord and that God would lift the burden on our family.

A week later, my mother's funeral was held at Shiloh Baptist Church in Henderson, North Carolina. My family had been members of Shiloh for over one hundred twenty years. Shiloh Baptist can accommodate five hundred people and the church was filled to capacity with people wanting to pay their respects to my mother. Family, relatives, friends, co-workers, and Wake Memorial Hospital's Chaplain came to pay respects to one of the most beautiful people the world has ever known.

I wrote a letter to the church and read it to the congregation. I wanted everyone to understand that all of us will one day go home to be with the Lord. I told the congregation that we are all better off for having known Martha Vann, and many people agreed with me. I was sad but I had an entire month to grieve prior to the funeral. I came into the realization of my own mortality, and I knew the key for me to continue on was to remain motivated about the possibilities God had for my family and me.

It was good to know my mother was not suffering anymore with her physical ailments. My mother is at peace now and I thank God for choosing Martha to be my mother—it's the greatest blessing that I know.

After my mother was buried, I prayed a lot because with her departure my concern centered on my father. Parkinson's Disease, diabetes, high blood pressure, and prostate issues were taking a toll. My dad was in remarkably good spirits considering he had his own health issues. Forty-two years of marriage, ten children, and fifteen grandchildren is noble work.

I said my goodbyes to family and friends, and drove back to Maryland. Being a member of a strong church made a significant difference in my resilience. I received a lot of support from day one of my mother's initial hospitalization.

While assigned to the budget directorate, I worked for Lieutenant Colonel Ben Marzette, an Air Force officer I had known from a previous military assignment. Ben is an outstanding man and a friend of mine. I appreciated all of his support throughout my tenure in the legislative branch of the budget shop.

Ben is the first African-American supervisor I ever had in the military. After thirteen years of duty, this was a long time coming. Lieutenant Colonel Howard Derrick was Chief of Budget Formulation at the time, and was the next level in my leadership chain.

Colonel Donna Taylor was the ANG Comptroller. She is one of my favorite people because her journey was not paved with gold; however, she was able to overcome adversity in her life and is one of the most successful officers in the United States Air Force. I have a lot of admiration for Donna Taylor and her family. Colonel Taylor and her husband are wonderful people.

Let me explain another one of the spiritual experiences I had. I went to the gym five days a week to keep my body in good physical condition. It was not unusual for me to arrive at the Pentagon Officer's Athletic Center (POAC) at 5:00 am to work out and jog. One morning, I decided to jog from the Pentagon, which is located in Virginia, to Capitol Hill, which is eight miles, round trip.

On one of those beautiful Washington, DC mornings I jogged past the Washington Monument, got closer to the steps of the Capitol building, and stopped. I stopped jogging because my inner voice let me know that one day I was going to be working on Capitol Hill. The words stuck in my head for the rest of my workout and I continued to try to figure out where it came from. A year later, I discovered what my spirit was telling me.

Lieutenant Colonel Marzette, Lieutenant Colonel Derrick and Ms. Rose Levea taught me how to interpret and analyze congressional inquires for Air Force and Capitol Hill legislative staffers. I discovered I had a passion for legislative work. My work on congressional inquiries opened up a vista of opportunity for my career.

I became a sponge in my efforts to learn about the legislative process, and I employed my academic success plan to my learning process. I read congressional language, researched each and every defense bill on record, and learned the name and committee of each member of Congress. My office also enrolled me in a number of courses hosted by Congressional Quarterly, Brookings Institute, and Georgetown University.

With each successive legislative course and/or class I

enrolled in, my passion for understanding how the legislative process worked grew even stronger. I was discovering a passion I otherwise wasn't aware of, and I was happy to be able to contribute to my organization.

My motivation in 1997 was to become the best officer in the military when it came to understanding the role of the legislative body and the armed services. My emphasis was squarely focused on how I could help the Air National Guard (ANG) obtain greater visibility on Capitol Hill and secure additional appropriation funding.

By increasing ANG's visibility, I could help over one hundred thousand men and women in the Air Guard do their jobs better. The ANG would receive additional funding to help procure the resources they needed in support of military readiness. In other words, more aircraft, equipment, comparable pay, benefits, and training opportunities (slots) at active duty Air Force leadership schools for officers and enlisted personnel.

I was motivated to help make the Air National Guard become the premier reserve component. I did not have to work very hard to carry the Air National Guard to the next level because Major General Donald Sheppard was at the helm. He was a visionary leader who knew how to get the job done while testifying on the Hill on behalf of the ANG. Kudos to Major General Sheppard for his contributions to the ANG and the Air Force—he is one of the best leaders the ANG has ever had.

In 1997, I applied for the Capitol Hill Fellowship Program, which is a program designed for promising Air Force, Air National Guard, and Air Force Reserve field grade officers. The Capitol Hill Fellowship Program allowed officers from the active duty and reserve components to work in the office of a member of Congress as a staffer to learn the legislative process while being an asset to the member's staff as a military expert.

I was highly motivated to make my mark in the legislative

arena, and I did by filling out the application for consideration to participate in the highly coveted fellowship program on Capitol Hill. Three weeks before the deadline date, I applied for the fellowship program and provided my branch chief with the application package, because I needed his approval before it went to the comptroller for signature.

On the evening of the deadline date, it was brought to my attention that instead of my fellowship package being forwarded to the comptroller, it was given to a civilian that worked on the staff. The next day the civilian thanked me for allowing him to copy my package. He copied my package verbatim except he used his name and the schools he had attended, and his reasons for wanting to participate was exactly as I wrote them three weeks earlier.

Our packages were then forwarded to the comptroller for signature and she forwarded them on to the interview board. My interview went very well, and the civilian and I were called in for a final interview. It finally came down to an interview with staff from the Brookings Institution, which was the collaborative host with Capitol Hill.

I went to the interview along with the civilian candidate, and all indications were that the decision would be made on the final selection in a week. In what seemed like a month, the decision came down and the civilian was selected to attend the fellowship program. I did not have a problem with this, except for the fact that the civilian used the exact words I wrote to justify his reasons for wanting to participate in the fellowship program.

A couple of months later, I requested a transfer to the National Guard Legislative Liaison Office to work as the Air Guard representative to Capitol Hill. Not only would I learn more about the legislative process, I would also be working directly with the Director of the ANG. This allowed me the opportunity to wear a suit to work every day. I worked with Capitol Hill personal and professional staffers to prepare and escort National Guard general officers to the Hill to meet with members of Congress.

Our office also supported the National Guard Association of the United States (NGAUS) annual conference. In 1997, I was one of the key action officers for the NGAUS conference, which meant I had to coordinate travel arrangements and hotel accommodations for all of the National Guard Bureau (NGB) staff. I had to ensure receipt of registration fees and meals for the flight. The conference was held in Albuquerque, New Mexico, which is a beautiful location.

The NGUAS Conference held in Albuquerque was also Major General Donald Shepherd's farewell address prior to retiring from the Air National Guard in January 1998. He was succeeded by Major General Paul Weaver as Director of the Air National Guard. I have to say over the course of my military career that I have had some of the best leadership America has to offer.

I am highlighting the significance of the NGAUS conferences because over three thousand soldiers and airmen attend the event, along with members of Congress, governors, local elected officials and candidates, and the President or Vice President of the United States. Networking at an event such as NGAUS is one of the primary activities that take place, and one can also obtain a sense of the direction one's organization is heading.

My duty as the ANG legislative liaison officer was going just great. I learned so much about the legislative process. I began attending courses on the Hill, many of which were taught by members of Congress. Georgetown University also hosted legislative classes on the Hill and would become the pipeline for the Capitol Hill Fellowship Program in 1998.

After seventeen years in the Air Force with ten years as an active duty officer and seven as an Active Guard Reservist with the ANG, I was coming into my own as a resource for the National Guard Bureau. I will tell any young officer or enlisted military person to continue to learn as much as you can about your particular area of expertise. My experience taught me that if you continue to be of service to your commander, branch chief, supervisor, or director, you will be called upon to do the impossible. You will be identified as a person who knows how to get the job done and in essence you become the go to person.

Likewise for men and women in private industry. If you learn as much as you can about your profession and the duties and responsibilities associated with your work, you will become the expert at your company and in your industry. I always enjoyed squeezing the blood out of the turnip in the sense that I asked every question that came to mind when it came to my job and industry. I left nothing to chance, and the people I worked for and with appreciated my tenacity when it came to knowing my job.

I was fortunate to work with outstanding leaders such as Lieutenant General Roger C. Schultz, Director Army National Guard. LTG Schultz commands over three hundred and fifty thousand Army soldiers and is an outstanding leader in the National Guard and the U.S. He and his wife are wonderful people and while on temporary duty with them they are very hospitable and genuine people. The Schultz's are great Americans.

Life really tests you during the times that things seem to be at their best in your life. In other words, when things are cranked up and going well, life has a way of balancing out by bringing us into reality. My reality occurred during the July 4th holiday in 1998, while visiting Henderson.

My sisters were caregivers for my father throughout the majority of my military career. It has been stated time and again God has angels in the earth and my five sisters Jacqueline, Gloria, Joan, Cynthia, and Tonya all shared in the caregiving of our father, Edward C. Vann.

They notified me that our father's health was taking a turn for the worse. Our father had Parkinson's Disease, high blood pressure, diabetes and a recent bout with prostrate surgery.

Our parents had symptoms most people in poverty have, especially in the African-American community.

My family made one of the toughest decisions we could make, and that was to put our father in an assisted living center. After speaking with my sisters about our father's condition, I visited him at the center, and he was in bad shape. My father recognized me; however, he was going in and out, meaning he was not as coherent and talkative as he normally would be. It really made me sad to see him in this condition, and I knew the inevitable was going to occur.

I always prayed for my parents and my family because God hears our prayers. I helped my father by shifting him in his hospital bed, and then I noticed the bed sores and I began to cry because there was blood on his bed sheets. So I asked the nurse for new sheets, and she accommodated us in this process. I believe in life that sometimes we see too much, and on this day I saw too much and threw myself down on my knees and prayed that God would not let my father suffer any longer.

Love of one's parents is like loving yourself. My mother and father didn't ask to grow up in poverty and experience a lifestyle filled with lack, yet they persevered with the dignity of people of royalty. I carry the noble blood of my mother and father and their parents before them. I am proud to say they are my parents just as I am their son; I was truly blessed to be raised by Martha and Cecil Vann.

After departing the assisted living center, I drove back to Maryland to get back to work. I was the key action officer for the 120th NGAUS General Conference, which was going to be held in Milwaukee, Wisconsin. I informed my supervisor of my father's condition, and he said that he would contact me if he received a call from my family.

On July 8, 1998, I flew from Washington, DC, to Milwaukee, Wisconsin, and checked into my hotel to prepare for meetings. I was negotiating rates with the hotel and taking a tour of the new convention center, which our organization was going to use while at the annual conference. I returned to my hotel room for the evening, reviewed my notes from the day's activities, and got a good night's rest.

The next morning, I visited with the alternate hotels for the three thousand attendees to negotiate rates with them and take a tour of the property. After finishing the morning review, I returned to the hotel I was staying in and the front desk told me to contact my office. I immediately returned to my room and my supervisor had contacted me, so I returned his call.

My supervisor informed me that I needed to contact my family in North Carolina because my father had passed away on the morning of July 9, 1998. Five days after I had visited my dad, he went home to be with the Lord. I packed my bag, checked out of the hotel, and flew back to Washington. After packing for the funeral, I contacted my family and drove to Henderson. All of my siblings made it back to our hometown. We met and prayed and cried and prayed some more.

The funeral at Shiloh Baptist Church was just as full as my mother's funeral had been. Over five hundred people took time out of their lives to pay their respects and say farewell. Numerous people attended, especially people from the local union he used to head as president of Bakery, Confectionary, and Tobacco (B.C.T.) Union Local #336T. Cecil was a champion for civil rights having lived by his mother's words "Stand up for your rights, before you lay down for your wrongs." He became an early leader and Shop Steward in 1967 for Local 336 T at the J.P. Taylor Tobacco Company and eventually became President for over 20 years. Cecil was also active in registering African-Americans to vote and served as precinct Captain for South Henderson, for the Democratic Party of North Carolina. He held active membership in the NAACP and the Beacon Light Masonic Lodge #249. Representatives from the North Carolina State American Federation of Labor and Congress of Industrial Organizations (AFL-CIO) sent representatives to thank our family for our father's service to the community, as well as people from Beacon Light Masonic Lodge #249.

My father completed the fourth grade and never received his high school diploma. My father and mother changed the world by their presence and sense of family and community. My dad gave his all for his family and community and my family loves him.

Oftentimes I think of what my father and mother must have experienced in society because of the hostility they confronted on their jobs each and every day. I could only imagine just how bad things were for them as individuals and as a couple when they applied for loans at a bank and were qualified to receive the money but were rejected because of the color of their skin.

My mother and father endured a lifetime of pain and sacrifice, and when I reflect on the outstanding job they did as parents, citizens, and community leaders, I say—job well done. My mother and father were inseparable, and they were two of the proudest Americans I have ever known. They defied the odds and moved into the future and were instrumental in shaping my life and the lives of my eight siblings.

I miss my mother and father and I still hold on to the fond memories we shared. God bless you, mom and dad, I love you. It's imperative to have faith at all times because inevitably we all lose our parents and it's never easy.

After saying my farewells to my family and the friends that attended my father's funeral, I returned to Washington, DC. Over the course of the nine consecutive years of being assigned to the Pentagon since 1990, over nine members of my family had passed away. Over thirteen family members had passed away by the time I retired from the Air Force.

In 1998, a year after applying for the Capitol Hill Fellowship Program, I was selected to fulfill a goal I had set for myself. Earlier I stated I was jogging on Capitol Hill when a voice on the inside of me stated I would be working on Capitol Hill. Well, it was my spirit letting me know I would be working on the Hill.

What a difference a year makes. I was honored to know that my supervisor supported me in my efforts to be selected to attend the Capitol Hill Fellowship Program. To this day, I am the first and only African-American military officer in the National Guard to attend the prestigious Capitol Hill Fellowship Program. I was very happy about my selection, and remaining motivated was the key to my success.

For example, had I given up on my dream to work on Capitol Hill, I would have considered myself a failure. Knowing I had the tenacity and the will to overcome my temporary setback let me know I was doing exactly what was meant for me all along. I thank God that my supervisor and the Air National Guard supported me, resulting in me having the experience of a lifetime.

ACTION PLAN #1

We All Need Keys to Open Doors to Success

MOTIVATION IS THE KEY TO OUR SUCCESS BECAUSE IT DEFINES our motive for wanting to succeed. Without motivation, we simply dangle from the key chains of life. With motivation, we can reach our military aspirations, whether as an officer or enlisted personnel.

Please list seven reasons why motivation is the key to your success. Narrow your choice to the one defining key to your future success and strive to achieve it.

1. _____

2. _____

3. _____

4. _____

5. _____

6. _____

7. _____

Motivation is the key to success because we have a defined reason for wanting to achieve goals. Successful people are self-motivated and don't need a lot of encouragement to see their dreams become reality. Successful people know exactly what they want in life and go after it like the intensity of the sun.

Motivation and drive have a direct correlation because it takes initiative and drive to succeed. We can mutually agree that over the course of our lives we work hard anyway; why not work hard serving our country?

When I think about motivation, it makes me think about the Wright Brothers. The Wright Brothers owned a bicycle shop in Dayton, Ohio, yet they were motivated to be the first people to fly a plane. The Wright Brothers tried and failed, tried and failed, but never gave up. They waited for the right weather conditions and finally propelled their aircraft into the sky. One could say the Wright Brothers were highly motivated.

ACTION PLAN #2

Got Motivation?

DO WE TRULY UNDERSTAND THE MOTIVATION BEHIND OUR success? Chances are there is a defining moment in our lives when someone or something inspired us to leave our comfort zone.

For those of us who are successful today, our memories are not so short that we have forgotten how we arrived at the destination called success. Follow me on this journey, and I will show you how I "Got Motivation."

It does not seem so long ago when I was in search of that elusive thing called success. I can recall one of those days when I was working hard to make ends meet and then someone or something came along and said something or wrote something profound that turned on a light inside of me. The figurative light that came on was my success catalyst, and then I came out of the darkness.

It is important for us to take a few minutes out of our busy schedules to reflect upon the person(s) or thing(s) that inspired us to leave our comfort zones so we could rediscover the light that led to our success.

For example, in 1996 I purchased the December issue of Success Magazine. The cover page read, "You Can Make Millions at Home, The Newest Way to Wealth." The article that inspired me to pursue my dream of becoming a motivational speaker was written by none other than motivational expert Brian Tracy. His article was titled, "Flood Your Life with Ideas."

After reading Brian Tracy's article, I left my comfort zone.

What motivated me most about Mr. Tracy was the fact that he revealed that at the age of sixteen, he dropped out of school. He was uninterested and unmotivated and earned money washing dishes and working in factories and at construction. At age twenty-one he left California and drove across the country. A few years later, on a ship out of Halifax, Nova Scotia, he went off to see the world and didn't return to the United States for ten years. By the time he was thirty, he had visited eighty countries and spoke four languages.

Tracy goes on to state, "While on a trip in Cape Town, South Africa, midway across the thousand-mile Sahara Desert the carburetor on his Land Rover broke down, then the steering rods and clutch. Tracy says, "I knew that if we couldn't fix the car his companions and he would die because they were running out of water." Tracy called upon skills he had picked up as a kid, repaired the vehicle, and the group made it across the desert.

Furthermore, Brian Tracy states, "That's when something locked in; I realized I was responsible for my own life. From that point on, I stopped blaming my parents, teachers, and other people. I knew nothing in my life would ever change unless I changed; I knew a person must be a proactive agent in his life rather than a reactive agent."

The following words from Brian Tracy's article stuck with me like glue, "You must be clear about the goals you set, flexible about the process of achieving them, and then continually learn all you can in every possible way to have success." I still have the article and will never throw it away because it still inspires me to this day.

It is important to understand that when Brian Tracy initially began his career as a professional speaker and seminar leader, he went to the edge of the cliff financially. In other words, Brian Tracy failed, yet the success catalyst for me was reading that he did not give up on his dream of achieving his goals and successes.

Brian Tracy's story is about how an entrepreneur who is flexible about the process of achieving his goals and is dedicated to continuous, lifelong learning can attain business success, despite a rocky, even disastrous start. By reading Brian Tracy's article, I "Got Motivation." Thanks, Mr. Brian Tracy.

Take a minute out of your busy schedule to recall the person(s) or thing(s) that inspired you to achieve success. Then you will have rediscovered how you "Got Motivation," and you will propel yourself to even greater success.

Please list seven people or things that contributed to your military success. By retracing our history we will rediscover our success catalysts, and achieve greater success in the future.

1. _____

2. _____

3. _____

4. _____

5. _____

6. _____

7. _____

*"Motivation is the key to success
when ordinary people are inspired to accomplish
extraordinary things in challenging times."*
—Paul Lawrence Vann

~ 8 ~

Capitol Hill:
the Experience of a Lifetime

*There is nothing more important than learning the art of
keeping your mind focused upon the things, conditions, and
circumstances of life that you really want.*
—Dennis Kimbro & Napoleon Hill

THE LOW POINT OF 1998 WAS LOSING MY FATHER; HE WAS THE
man who taught me perseverance. Now that mom and dad
were no longer on the earth, I knew it was time to reach deep
down on the inside of me for the resilience my parents taught my
eight siblings and me. The Capitol Hill Fellowship Program sustained me through the loss of my departed loved ones because it
offered a fresh start, a new beginning. The Fellowship Program
helped me chart a new course in my career aspirations.

The purpose of the Air Force Legislative Fellowship Program
is to provide highly qualified officers possessing proven leadership potential with an intense exposure to the processes,
procedures, and culture of the United States Congress. Fellows
receive hands-on experience to develop a working knowledge
of the operations of Congress. Officers in the rank of Major
work one full year on Capitol Hill with a full-time assignment
on the staff of a member of Congress; they also attend periodic
seminars with the Government Affairs Institute at Georgetown
University staff throughout the fellowship year.

Responsibilities of a Fellow include legislative research, writing, analysis, briefings, and general problem-solving, primarily in the areas of national defense, intelligence, and veterans affairs. After the Air Force notified me of my report date, I had to select members in either the Senate or House I was interested in working with, and schedule appointments with them.

I was very familiar with both Houses of Congress because of the experience I attained as ANG's legislative liaison officer. I immediately opened my 106th Congressional Directory to select the member offices I would contact for prospective interviews for the fellowship program.

Members of the Senate I contacted included: Senator Kay Bailey Hutchinson, Texas; Senator Trent Lott, Mississippi; Senator Thad Cochran, Mississippi; and Senator Sam Brownback, Kansas.

Members of the House of Representatives I contacted include: Representative Bill Young, Florida; Representative James Gibbons; Nevada; and Representative Patrick Kennedy, Rhode Island.

After consistent and intense interviews with numerous members of Congress who primarily served on armed services committees, the best fit for me came during my interview with William "Bill" Burke, Legislative Director for Congressman Patrick J. Kennedy of Rhode Island.

Upon entering the office of Congressman Kennedy, I was greeted by Ms. Terri Alford, Executive Assistant. Terri has a wonderful personality, and I knew from my initial conversation with her that I would enjoy working on Representative Kennedy's staff. When it comes to beautiful people, Terri is at the top of the list.

Another wonderful member of Representative Kennedy's staff is Ms. Kimber Colton. Kimber has a law degree, is very intelligent, and understands the legislative process very well. Kimber and I worked on a number of military-related issues.

I assisted Kimber with a meeting pertaining to NATO Peace Keeping Operations with international students from the Navy Legal School located in Rhode Island. My military background helped immeasurably, and my presentation to the students resulted in a lot of questions from the students, which made the meeting even more productive. Kimber and her husband Jason are wonderful people and my family enjoys going to brunch with them. My daughter Paula Marie loves being around Kimber.

Brian Vigue was a legislative assistant working on Representative Kennedy's staff. Brian was techno savvy and taught me a lot about legislative research. Brian was a sharp staffer, and knew how to get the wheels turning when it came to getting legislation moving through the process. Brian and I became and still are very good friends. Brian and his wife Carla are very nice people, and they welcomed me to their home as if I were a member of their family. Brian and Carla moved back to Wisconsin to be near their family.

Matt Braunstein was a sharp legislative assistant working for Representative Kennedy, and he understood policy issues quite well. Matt also earned his master's degree from Georgetown University, which was a feat in and of itself, considering the demands and responsibilities while working on the Hill.

Meghan Boyle was a legislative assistant who had recently graduated from college. She was sharp when it came to understanding the legislative process. Meg kept me honest, meaning she was always very helpful and had a great personality and was fun to be around. Meg went on to law school so I know I will learn more great things about her in the near future. Way to go, Meg.

William (Bill) Burke interviewed me, and he was a very meticulous individual. Bill was as sharp as they come in understanding the legislative process. During our interview, he did a wonderful job getting me to answer his questions. It was a win-win situation for Congressman Kennedy's staff and me.

I knew I wanted to work with Bill from the very beginning.

After the interview, I had a very good feeling about receiving a follow-up call to work as the military legislative assistant, and less than a week later I received the call I hoped to get. I enjoyed working for Bill.

I enjoyed working for Bill because he knew the legislative business inside-out. Bill taught me a lot about the legislative process. Bill and his wife are very good people, and I admired him.

While on assignment as a legislative assistant for Congressman Kennedy, a lot of people asked me what it was like to work on his personal staff and what he was like. I can honestly say I had the experience of a lifetime because I was allowed to flourish. For example, I developed a calendar to address all armed services, intelligence, and veteran issues which helped Representative Kennedy and his staff stay apprised of all House Armed Services Committee (HASC) full and subcommittee meetings and votes.

My inputs and insight assisted the Congressman on key armed services votes that affected our men and women in uniform and their families. I assisted in the drafting and bipartisan support for house resolution (H.R.) 2283, a bill to amend title ten, United States Code, to improve the authorities relating to the provision of honor guard details at funerals of veterans.

Congressman Patrick J. Kennedy is a very humble man, and I saw this humility in him each and every day. Patrick is a good man, and I respect him for being the person he is. I appreciated him and his staff for teaching me how the legislative process works and treating me with dignity. I will go on record to say of the twenty Air Force Fellows on Capitol Hill, I had the best experience, because I was an Air National Guard Legislative Liaison officer prior to my Hill assignment.

My previous experience working with members and staff gave me an advantage in knowing what to expect, and I capitalized on the opportunity to learn even more while in the fellowship program.

I will also go on to say that I worked with numerous interns during my year on the Hill and they were positive energy for me and the staff. Mind you, I was one of the oldest personal staffers in Congressman Kennedy's office, but it balanced itself out because when you add youth and experience together, typically you get positive results. I thoroughly enjoyed my Capitol Hill experience, and made a lot of friends that I communicate with to this day.

One of the most interesting experiences for me was to receive an assignment from Bill, who was the Legislative Director, which involved contacting Pentagon officials. Whenever I called the Pentagon I informed the staff that I was a Capitol Hill Fellow, and after telling them this, they would assist me with no problem. If by chance someone called the Congressman's office on an armed services issue, they thought I was a permanent member of the Congressman's personal staff.

Meeting with veteran service organizations (VSO) from Rhode Island was one of my favorite things to do. They come to Washington for conferences and stop in to visit their representatives and know their issues thoroughly. I must tell you the VSO's are sharp and know what they need, and I enjoyed every minute of the meetings.

I represented Congressman Kennedy at HASC meetings to obtain better insight to key issues projected for full committee meetings, and apprised Bill or the Congressman on major legislation affecting the military services, intelligence, or veterans.

As mentioned earlier, I had a very good reputation for working Hill issues while assigned to the National Guard Bureau. During the first month of the Fellowship, I was attending a HASC subcommittee meeting and one of the committee staffers asked me what was I doing attending their meeting.

In other words, he did not know I was a Capitol Hill Fellow, and at that point I laughed because it meant I was fully integrated into the legislative system—he assumed I was taking the liberty to sit in on their meeting. He and I laughed at that incident because it proved that I was effective from my military position at the National Guard Bureau prior to the fellowship beginning. Working for Patrick was a powerful experience.

Patrick Kennedy is the son of Senator Ted Kennedy and the nephew of President John F. Kennedy. He comes from an outstanding family—I respect the Kennedy's for who they are and what they represent. I did not have a personal agenda while working for him, nor would I have had one working for another member of Congress.

All I know is that my spirit communicated to me that I would be working on Capitol Hill some day, and the inner voice I mentioned earlier directed my path. Obviously, God had something he wanted me to do on the Hill and I believe I have helped people in the process. I admire Representative Kennedy. I met his family at his birthday party, and they are more wonderful than you will ever know. I had the most wonderful experience in my life working for Congressman Patrick J. Kennedy. Of the twenty years of military service, the Hill experience was the most rewarding because it helped me learn how the legislative process works.

I also worked with members of the Senate and Senate staffers and the entire New England Caucus, and it was fabulous. I learned a lot about how delegations work, and how collaborations help districts and the state as a whole. The legislative branch of our government is important to our republic, and I can say I learned a lot during my one-year fellowship assignment.

I want everyone to remember the following, "If you do what you love, you will never work another day in your life." My year on Capitol Hill was not like work because I loved what I was doing. Please don't misunderstand me, working on Capitol Hill is hard work and the people who do this every day are to be commended for their efforts. If you don't believe that people work hard on the Hill, then I recommend you try it for a year.

You will be amazed at the energy level required to help make the wheels of government turn in our country.

In 1999, I received a phone call from the Air National Guard personnel office, and the individual asked me, "Are you sitting down?" It was like déja vu all over again. In fact, I was sitting at my desk answering constituent mail; this meant I was busy taking care of Rhode Island constituents. The sergeant stated, "Major Vann, you have been promoted to the rank of Lieutenant Colonel."

There was silence, and I almost fell out of my chair, but I remained composed for a second or two. Then I screamed, "Yes!" The sergeant laughed and stated, "You are now a Lieutenant Colonel in the Air National Guard." I said thank you for the call and I thought about my mother and father and I was on cloud nine floating like a butterfly.

I contacted Colonel Davis, my supervisor at the National Guard Bureau legislative office to thank him for supporting me, and then I informed Congressman Kennedy's personal staff of the great news. Congressman Kennedy's staff recommended I hold the promotion and rank pinning ceremony on the Hill. We were also able to reserve the Small Business Committee room and it was grand.

I contacted the National Guard Bureau to find out which general officer would be available to officiate the promotion ceremony; however, no one was available. Congressman Kennedy stated he would be honored to host the promotion ceremony, and I was elated. Then Colonel Donna Taylor, ANG Comptroller, assisted along with Colonel Bruce Davis and Colonel Jim Thompson.

Over one hundred people attended my promotion ceremony. My sister Gloria and her husband represented my family, along with my Uncle John Hawkins and Aunt Virginia Hawkins and their daughter Jennifer from New York. My relatives from Indianapolis and Cincinnati also attended—Jo Osili,

Clara Banks, Francis McKinney and her daughter Kara. After picking up my cousins from Washington Reagan Airport, my cousin Clara slipped and fell, and we took her to the hospital. Fortunately, she was alright and we were able to make it back to the Hill on time. We all arrived on Capitol Hill an hour prior to the promotion ceremony. Then the caterers delivered the food—I was going all out on this promotion party. The caterers did an excellent job and the food was very good.

The protocol staff from the National Guard Bureau did an excellent job. I remember Captain Kim Greene reading the orders and then it was time for the pinning ceremony. Colonel Taylor presented me with the meritorious service medal (MSM) with two Oak Leaf Clusters. Congressman Kennedy pinned the Lieutenant Colonel rank on my right shoulder, and Colonel Thompson pinned the rank on my left shoulder, and after repeating the oath I was officially a Lieutenant Colonel in the Air National Guard.

I worked across the hall from Congressman Jessie Jackson, Jr., thus he and his staff attended the ceremony along with the other nineteen Capitol Hill Fellows. Staff from the Government Affairs Institute at Georgetown University attended, as well as many of my friends from the National Guard Bureau.

All of my supervisors over the past nine years attended my promotion ceremony. When I looked outside the window of the Small Business Committee room in the Cannon House Office Building, I knew my parents were looking down at the ceremony from the heavens. Everything I owe, I owe to Martha and Cecil Vann. My promotion to Lieutenant Colonel belongs to my parents.

The day after my promotion, I had to leave my relatives at my house in Maryland because there were votes on the floor of the House and I needed to track them in order to update Representative Kennedy. I began to understand the legislative process better and better, and I could follow the links to a bill simply by focusing on the author of a given bill and the legislative language attached to it.

As a result of working on the staff of a member on the House Armed Services Committee (HASC), I was a part of the authorization committee process. With the congressional cycle coming to an end, it was time to shift my thinking to the appropriations committee to ensure sufficient funding in support of the Congressman's district in Providence and Newport, Rhode Island, where the Navy War College and Naval Undersea Warfare Center are located. I learned more about the Navy, Marines, and Merchant Marines in one year than I had learned over the course of my entire military career.

The Congressman's staff had concerns pertaining to downsizing of shipyards because issues of downsizing would affect the shipyards in Rhode Island. The Navy was focusing their efforts on right sizing the number of ships for our nation's defense.

Issues such as first responders made it into legislation; however, the funding had not been provided during my tenure on the Hill. The Balkans War was being managed by the Air Force, and concern about the use of ground forces was making news—a ground war was too risky at the time.

Congressman Chris Cox's intelligence report hit the streets and our relationship with China was making headlines. One of my favorite people, General Krulak, Commandant of the Marine Corps, visited Congressman Kennedy's office. He came to thank Representative Kennedy for supporting legislation to provide cold weather gear for his Marines. He was quite a leader. General Krulak had an infectious personality and you could feel his sincerity whenever you were in his presence.

I always came to work early because I didn't like sitting in traffic. Even though I lived only six miles from Capitol Hill, I always left home at 6 a.m. because I could get a lot done before anyone else arrived in the office.

My year on the Hill seemed to be going by very fast. On

one day in particular, the phone rang and I answered it as I normally did by stating, "Hello, you have reached the office of Congressman Patrick J. Kennedy, and how may I help you today?" The individual answered, "Good morning, this is John Kennedy, Patrick's cousin. May I speak to him?"

I said, "Hello, John, I hope all is well with you," and he said everything was fine. I told him I was in the Capitol Hill Fellowship program, and he said I hope to meet you in the near future, and I said that would be great. This phone conversation took place three weeks before the unfortunate plane crash that took the life of three young Americans.

The morning after the crash I happened to be at the Pentagon Officers Athletic Center working out in the gym. I was riding the stationary bike, warming up as I normally did, then all of a sudden an up-to-the-minute news report came on TV, and the announcer stated that John Kennedy, Jr.'s plane was missing. The passengers on the plane included his wife Carolyn Bessette Kennedy, his sister in-law Lauren Bessette, and of course John Jr.

If anyone on the Kennedy staff could understand the passing of loved ones, it was me. I served over twelve consecutive years in the Pentagon, and my family lost thirteen family members from January 1990 through October 2002, when I retired. God knew my family because we were always before him at another funeral and we asked him to relieve our burdens. Continuous prayer is the only way to deal with losing a loved one, and I prayed that God would lift the burden of the Bessette and Kennedy families.

Even though I never met John F. Kennedy, Jr., I knew I would have liked him because he was an interesting man. Many African-Americans admired his father and family. I will always remember walking into my parents' and grandparents' house and looking at the pictures of President Kennedy and Dr. Martin Luther King, Jr. hanging on the wall. I can also say the same thing about other families throughout my community. We had a lot of respect for the Kennedy family, and since John Jr. was a member of the family, we admired him and his family.

Congressman Kennedy's office received an outpouring of sympathy and condolences from all over the world, and the constituents in his district were very warm and sensitive to Patrick and his family in this time of loss. Events such as this always remind me to pray every day because we don't know the time or the place we are going to leave this world.

I have a copy of George Magazine, and I like a quote John wrote: "If we can do just one thing at George, we hope it's to demystify the political process, to enable you to see politicians not just as ideological symbols but as lively and engaging men and women who shape public life." Amen John, Amen.

Another seminal event occurred while working for Congressman Kennedy that many of you will recall as well. Typically, when I arrived in the office early, I would complete work assignments I needed to close out, then I would go on the internet to read the headlines. On one morning in particular, I happened to see that Senator Chafee had died. I had met Senator Chafee on a number of occasions because I attended several meetings with him, and I admired him.

Congressman Kennedy's office worked with Senator Chafee on a daily basis because they worked on behalf of the entire constituency in Rhode Island. I printed a copy of the news release and gave a copy to the member's staff and we were all saddened about the senator's death. The compassion and outpouring for Senator Chafee resonated into Representative Kennedy's office, and to the citizens of Rhode Island.

My Capitol Hill experience was an experience of a lifetime. One day Brian Vigue and I visited the Senate because Senator John McCain was heading the Senate Boxing Commission, and we knew Muhammad Ali would be testifying about the impact boxing has on athletes. Brian didn't bring his camera, so he decided to leave and purchase one in the Senate store. Minutes later, none other than Muhammad Ali walked out of the Senate hearing room.

I walked up to Muhammad Ali and shook his hand and said hello and he smiled that wonderful smile and said hello. In just a few minutes he was surrounded by admiring fans. Brian returned with his camera, but it was too late because the crowd was getting larger and larger. Brian gave me a hard time about missing the opportunity to meet Ali, and yet I was able to meet him and to shake hands with him.

Working for Congressman Patrick J. Kennedy was a wonderful experience, filled with numerous opportunities for learning, and that's exactly why I enjoyed my year on Capitol Hill. Prior to completing my fellowship, I was enrolled in the Legislative Studies program at the Government Affairs Institute at Georgetown University.

Many of my classes were conducted on Capitol Hill by Georgetown staff. I was enrolled in classes such as Congress and National Security and Congress and Money. I wrote my paper and presented my speech on Asymmetric Threats and attacks on the United States. Little did I know how much our country would change after I finished the Capitol Hill Fellowship program.

The Capitol Hill Fellowship Program graduation ceremony was held at the Republican National Committee Headquarters on the Hill, and all twenty Air Force Fellows received their certificates from their Congressman's or Senator's office. The staff at Georgetown did a great job managing the program, and all twenty of us departed for our follow-up assignments.

Only in America can a poor, young, African-American man be given a chance to live his dream working on Capitol Hill. Thank God and thank America.

ACTION PLAN #1

Get Actively Involved in the Political Process

I, FOR ONE, DECIDED YEARS AGO I WOULD NEVER RUN FOR public office. I experienced first hand the demands of a member of Congress during my Capitol Hill Fellowship Program in 1998-99. Being a member of Congress is the ultimate in public service, but not for me. I advocate all citizens in the U.S. become actively involved in public service because it's a liberating experience, and you can learn a lot about the legislative process.

The only thing more important than voting is to understand what we are voting for. Before I became politically astute, I didn't always understand the issues or policies; many of us don't. Now I know exactly what I am voting for and why. We should all know why we are voting for certain initiatives and for our elected officials.

If we don't understand what our elected officials stand for, then we should start attending hearings or meetings to get a better perspective of their philosophy. Likewise, if we don't understand an initiative that is going to change how we live, we should start asking questions.

Please list seven things you would like to learn about the legislative process. Once you list them, call or email your elected official's district office or Capitol Hill office to get the answers you are seeking. Enjoy the experience—after all, you likely helped vote your member into office.

1. _____

2. _____

3. _____

4. _____

5. _____

6. _____

7. _____

ACTION PLAN #2

Our Military Personnel Should Understand the Importance of Voting

THE 2004 PRESIDENTIAL ELECTION WAS ANOTHER EXCITING event in our nation's history. Citizens inside and outside our borders voted by absentee ballot or stood in line to vote at the polling booths—especially military personnel.

Of the 295 million citizens in the U.S., approximately 144 million were eligible to vote. The voter turnout was high. Prior to voting, I decided to review my "Official Election Mail" for the fourth time.

My election mail was distributed by the county board of elections. It read as follows: "Tuesday, November 2, 2004 is the date for the upcoming General Election. This is the day that we vote for the national, state, and local officials who will represent us. All registered citizens are registered to vote."

It goes on to state, "We urge you to participate in the electoral process. This is an opportunity for you to take an active part in shaping the future of our country. You will vote for candidates who will be setting policy affecting all citizens in the country. Don't sit idly by. Encourage your registered family, friends, and neighbors to vote on November 2, 2004." It was signed the President of the Board of Elections.

My motivation for voting stems from my childhood. My mother and father were two of the most avid voters I have ever known. Just how passionate were my parents about voting? By the time my parents went to vote, they could explain the issues to all nine of their children, because they knew the issues would be impacting us.

After my eighteenth birthday, the first thing my parents encouraged me to do was to register to vote. When Election Day arrived, my parents drove my older sister and I to the school where we voted.

Even after my parent's health began to decline in their later years, they still insisted they wanted to register and vote, because this was their opportunity to take an active part in the shaping of our country. My parents' example resonates with all nine of their children to this day, and I am proud to say I voted in the recent election.

Perhaps your motivation is different from mine or maybe it's the same. I am an American and I don't take my right to vote for granted. I know we are all motivated to vote because we understand freedom, liberty, and most importantly, hope for our future.

To those of us who are parents, we need to help our children understand the importance of voting in America. I am truly blessed to have parents who led by example when it came to voting. We are all blessed to be living in the United States of America. I love America, and I know we are motivated to vote in future elections. I will learn more about the election process by speaking with my voting representative in my chain of command because: _____

_____

_____

∽ 9 ∽

Achieving Unparalleled Excellence

It all starts with self. When you change yourself, then you can change the world a little bit. By expanding your self-awareness, you are becoming more familiar and intimate with the field of infinite possibilities that exists within you. Once you've become that, then you begin to change the world.

—Dr. Deepak Chopra

CONGRESSMAN KENNEDY REQUESTED AN EXTENSION SO I COULD work in his office for six additional months; however, my military leadership required my services and I returned to my duty station. In January, 2000, I reported to the National Guard Bureau legislative liaison office and met with my supervisor. He directed me to work in the National Guard Policy and Liaison Branch.

I worked for a civilian by the name of Larry Tech, who was a GS-14 in the federal government and an Army National Guard Colonel (Ret.) officer. Mr. Tech was a solid citizen, highly respected throughout the National Guard Bureau, and a great man to work for and with. What I appreciated most about working for Larry was his willingness to teach what he knew. Larry knew a lot about the National Guard, leadership, and getting the job done the right way.

Larry had a small staff, which included Major Lynette Hupman; Senior Master Sergeant Blaine Ross; and me.

Eventually, our branch increased in size; however, it occurred after Mr. Tech retired from civil service.

Unfortunately, Larry retired due to complicated health problems; he was a great person to work for. After he retired from civil service, I took over the duties of the National Guard Policy Office. We were charged with the responsibility to ensure all regulations were updated, as well as new policies from the Army and Air Force. Then my staffed vetted policies to Lieutenant General Russell Davis, Chief National Guard, and the Directorates of the Army and Air National Guard.

Staffing regulations is a full-time responsibility for the Policy Branch staff and we performed our duties very well. Major issues such as Military Funeral Honor Duties, Anthrax Vaccine for soldiers and airmen, and the annual Reserve Forces Policy Board inputs took on more defined meaning after we decided the impact the policies would have on National Guard personnel.

I really enjoyed the work because we assembled working groups for each of our major policies. This meant we collaborated with the National Guard Judge Advocate General, Comptroller personnel, Human Resources, Project Managers, Morale, Welfare, and Recreation (MWR) experts, and a host of technical experts—professional and hardworking men and women.

Looking back on my experience in the Policy Branch, it was a lot of fun because I could see the results of our efforts. My staff and I received a lot of exposure because we brought key policy issues to the forefront for the National Guard. One of our major projects was the OM 10-5, the National Guard's organization and responsibilities manual for the National Guard Bureau and the Army and Air National Guard.

The OM 10-5 had not been revised for quite a few years; thus, the Policy Branch was tasked to update and revise the document. We had to obtain signatures from every organization throughout the National Guard, and we did it. Eventually, it was signed by the Chief of the National Guard Bureau.

The bottom line is that my branch was given a challenging task to accomplish. We worked together and made it happen against all odds. By accomplishing the impossible, we were able to garner support from our entire organization of twelve hundred people in the National Guard Bureau, because we all agreed on the substance of the document. In essence, we revised the organizational doctrine for the entire National Guard, which totals over half a million people throughout the United States, Territories, and Possessions.

No one can ever tell me something is impossible, because my staff and I experienced and saw the results of our efforts. People like Master Sergeant Mark Downing, Captain Jay Watts, and Bruno Leuyer helped make the project successful through their efforts. The top leadership of the National Guard signed off and approved of the OM 10-5 Organizations and Responsibilities document. The approval of the National Guard organizational doctrine occurred because everyone openly communicated the goal of the project, and were accountable for their actions. In my estimation, it was one of the greatest feats ever accomplished in the National Guard.

The OM10-5 was one of the greatest feats in the National Guard because leadership, management, and staff were willing and able to openly identify what their roles and missions consist of for their organization, and then they put it in writing. That's why the document is a living and breathing instrument to this day. Doctrine is one of the most important criteria for any organization; it's the lifeblood, especially for a military organization. Bravo National Guard, Bravo!

I became the National Guard's expert on the Annual Reserve Forces Policy Board (RFPB), which meant I had to analyze and review Army, Air and Joint Staff inputs and obtain Chief Guard Bureau coordination of RFPB prior to disseminating it to the RFPB Board.

The RFPB is a great project, and it was fun for me because it was never boring. We provided profiles supporting National Guard operation and maintenance funding, and equipment and personnel funding totals for the entire fiscal year. I enjoy seeing teams work together because it means people are excelling, and I saw a lot of people working to ensure the proper information was going to be reviewed by the RFPB, Department of Defense and Congress.

Achieving unparalleled excellence ultimately means individuals are readily surrendering their unique individual abilities for the good of the organization and its progress. I can say unequivocally that no one learned as much or capitalized on opportunities more than I did because I always took an all or nothing approach to my work, career field, and organizational interests.

I always wanted to be on the best team, work with the best organization, and provide the best customer service to everyone I was involved with. There were times when I fell short, because people and or organizations don't agree with you all of the time. I was highly motivated to make a difference in the lives of those around me.

Throughout the course of my lifetime, people have always considered me to be a very positive person—very upbeat, with an infectious smile and can-do attitude. For the most part, it stems from my vision of wanting a better life and world around me. For example, over the course of my personal and professional life I have been given countless opportunities to work on committees as the chairman or as a volunteer and the interactions with people from all parts of the world have shaped my perspective of humanity.

When I look for the answer to my success, my parents ensured that my siblings and I had respect for other people. It's really amazing when I think about it, various issues I thought were so important really weren't. The most important aspect of being a military officer was my drive to always do my very best, to make my leadership look good. My goal was to always make a positive impression on an otherwise hopeless situation, and most of the time, the key issues standing between the success of a project and failure was people and/or an organization not wanting positive change.

I, for one, can honestly say the Army National Guard, Air National Guard, and the Joint Staff strive to be the best at what they do. The Guard has a long history of service to our country and today it's no different; they know how to get the job done and done right. I served ten years in the Air Force, and ten years in the Air National Guard as an Active Guard Reservist (AGR), and I've worked with all branches of the military. The National Guard is a world-class organization.

Some of my interest outside of the National Guard included the Olympic Games. My dream of becoming an Olympic 400-meter runner for the United States never materialized. I have always enjoyed track and field, and will follow it for the rest of my life. In July 2000 I flew to Sacramento, California, for the Olympic Trials to see American track and field athletes compete for a slot on the team.

Even though McClelland Air Force Base was projected to close in less than a year, I was able to obtain lodging at the billeting office, which wasn't far from the campus of Sacramento (SAC) State College where the Olympic Trials are held.

SAC State provides an excellent venue for track and field, and there were huge crowds for each competition at the Olympic trials.

My favorite athlete for the 2000 Olympic team was Marion Jones. I met her and was able to get her to autograph my 2000 Olympic Trials tee shirt as well as to autograph her book, *See How She Runs*. Jackie Joyner Kersey, also one of my favorites, obliged me with her autograph as well.

I attended the 1996 Olympic Trials in Atlanta, and they were held at what is now the home of the Atlanta Braves baseball team. Michael Johnson, the 400-meter champ from 1996, was my favorite male athlete and his showdown in the 200 meters with Maurice Greene was going to be the highlight of the trials competition. However, neither qualified because they were injured during the 200 finals.

One can say I am a fan of the Olympics and just because I didn't realize my dream on the track, I could still participate as a volunteer at the 2000 Olympic Trials. The Sacramento Sports Commission offered local travel packages to surrounding areas, and I selected Lake Tahoe and San Francisco as my two travel destinations.

I didn't know anyone on the bus prior to riding to Lake Tahoe; however, before the trip ended, I met and became friends with some great people. One man in particular was Howard Schmertz. Howard is the meet director for the Millrose Games, which is a track and field meet held in Madison Square Garden each year. Howard is the son of the original meet director for the Millrose Games, Fred Schmertz.

I enjoyed meeting Howard and some of the volunteers and judges who supported the Games for decades. I took a picture with Howard while we were riding a boat on Lake Tahoe. I enjoyed the insight he provided regarding the Olympics, and volunteering in particular. To be honest with you, he inspired me to research how to get involved in the Olympic Games movement. Mr. Schmertz, thanks for your inspiration. The next day, I took a trip to San Francisco and enjoyed that beautiful city—especially the restaurants at the pier. What a city!

After the Olympic Trials ended I flew back to Washington, DC, and made plans to attend the 2000 Olympic Games in Sydney, Australia. Tickets for the airline trip and events were still available; however, my schedule was too busy.

I was a friend of and worked with Willie Davenport, who

was a five-time Olympian. Willie and I worked at the National Guard Bureau, and I spoke with him while in Sacramento during the trials. He told me volunteering is a good way to get involved in the Olympic movement. Willie was a Colonel in the Army National Guard and he was a great officer, leader, and man. Unfortunately Colonel Davenport succumbed to a heart attack while traveling through O'Hare Airport after a conference and passed away, and we all miss his great spirit.

The year 2001 is almost upon me and I am about to reach my nineteenth year of military service. I have been assigned to the Pentagon for over eleven consecutive years. I had to make a decision to retire in a year, or continue to pursue my professional military career in the National Guard for more leadership opportunities.

The Policy Branch of the National Guard Bureau was part of the Joint Staff during my tenure. We were responsible for "All States Memorandums." All States Memos are policy documents developed and staffed throughout the Army, Air, and Joint Staff of the National Guard Bureau and electronically disseminated to every National Guard State Headquarters, Territory, Possession and the District of Columbia.

Issues such as Department of Defense policy pertaining to anthrax vaccines for Army and Air Guard soldiers and airmen, retiree flags, military funeral honor duty, annual conferences, and human resource issues were vetted through my office prior to coordination with the directors of the Army, Air, Joint Staff and Chief of the National Guard Bureau.

In the Policy Branch, we were responsible for providing oversight for policies, regulations, and every written or electronic document in the National Guard. We served over half a million military personnel and civilians working for the National Guard.

What gave me the most satisfaction as Policy Branch Chief was observing the stellar performance of my staff. They did an exceptional job against all odds. Policy work is not as sexy as legislative liaison work; however, without current, accurate, and properly vetted policies in place, an organization as large as the National Guard could easily be paralyzed by the very policies, regulations, and guidance they needed to adhere to in support of national security.

Many officers and enlisted personnel would prefer to work in support of Capitol Hill initiatives because it's sexier. I thank all of the personnel who worked for and with me, and the working groups that formed and developed on behalf of a better and more productive National Guard.

The National Guard, including leadership, staff, personnel, and civilians, is a world class organization making a tremendous contribution to the United States of America maintaining its freedom, liberty, and hope for a better America in the future.

ACTION PLAN #1

Don't Be Afraid to Succeed

SOMETIMES WE CARRY BAGGAGE IN OUR MENTAL LUGGAGE, OR shall we say minds. The most dangerous item in our mental luggage is our fear of success. Show me a person afraid to succeed and I will show you a person that has a self-defeating attitude. The solution for overcoming fear of success is to fill our daily lives with prayer, positive affirmations, positive self-help books, and confidence exercises. I espoused these tenets to our military personnel because they have the distinction of going into harm's way. Trust me, don't worry about what others say; pray because it can keep you alive.

Please list seven additional solutions to help someone you know or yourself overcome self-defeating thoughts, actions, environments, and lifestyles. We are all winners and should think like winners.

1. _____

2. _____

3. _____

4. _____

5. _____

6. _____

7. _____

Unfortunately, no one can change their childhood; however, they can change their future. It's incumbent upon everyone to believe in their dreams in order to experience success. At times people bring negative childhood experiences into adulthood, not realizing it paralyzes their personal and professional relationships.

After discussing my plans of becoming a motivational speaker with a close friend of mine, he looked me straight in the eye and said, "You will not be able to do that." I asked him if he had ever spoken professionally, and he said no. So I asked him, "What makes you think I won't become a professional speaker?" and he said,"I don't know." If I had listened to him, I wouldn't be living my dreams. It's important for us to stay away from toxic people.

ACTION PLAN #2

Having the Courage to Aim High, Then Higher

WE ALL AT SOME TIME OR OTHER ARE PRESENTED WITH CHAL-LENGES in life. Some of them are personal, while others may be professional in origin. We must understand how to call upon our reserves, which is courage.

In order to succeed at what we love (duty, honor, country) we must summon the courage and conviction to carry us to victory on our missions in life. Courage doesn't always have to be big and bold; it can be small and unassuming. For example, if we happen to be in pursuit of a promotion, it takes courage to sit down and talk to our supervisors or managers about it.

If our next promotion is determined by whether we completed a leadership school, finished a degree, or took command, it takes time and courage to balance our military duties, schoolwork, and family at the same time. Courage is needed in all capacities whether we realize it or not.

It certainly takes a lot of courage to start and finish a lifelong goal. If our goal is our dream, have big courage and it will pay off in the end. Whenever we aim high, then higher, to reach our dream of dreams we are simply adding a layer of courage. You may be asking yourself how do I know this. It's simple, I'll explain it to you.

When we wake up each morning we assume everything is going to work out perfectly. All of our planning and all of our meetings leading up to showtime never guarantees success. Even though there are no guarantees in life, we still have the courage to get up the following morning and try it again, because we know if we stop reaching for success we will never realize it.

Please write down seven courageous things you need to accomplish this month. Compare your list with your results and see how well you do. Repeat your courage list each month and you will realize just how courageous you really are.

1. _____

2. _____

3. _____

4. _____

5. _____

6. _____

7. _____

$\sim$ 10 $\sim$

Be Willing to Go After
Your Dreams

*Well, at some point in time, I began to see the audience as part of
my very own support system. I don't know when it happened, but
I'll tell you this: When it happened, for the first time in my career,
I stopped talking at people and started talking with them.*

—Bill Gove

THE SUMMER OF 2001 WAS GOING TO BE THE BEST SUMMER ON
record for me. Even though I was unable to attend the 2000
Olympics in Sydney, Australia, I decided to attend the 2001
Goodwill Games in Brisbane, Australia. I wanted to spend my
birthday in Australia, and besides, I wanted to meet people in
the Olympic movement and the Goodwill Games would provide the forum for such meetings.

One of my goals for visiting Brisbane was to meet officials
in the Olympic movement, to learn as much as I could about
international sporting events, and by 2004 be in a position
to participate as a volunteer in the 2004 Olympics in Athens,
Greece—the home of the modern Olympics.

After obtaining approval from my supervisor, I purchased
my airline ticket and hotel accommodations. I meticulously
selected the events I planned on viewing once I arrived in
Brisbane. I departed Baltimore on August 31, 2001, and flew
to Los Angeles for my twelve-hour layover. Once I arrived in
Los Angeles, I rented a car, checked into an airport hotel to get

more sleep, then tour Los Angeles and eat at Spagos, Wolfgang Puck's restaurant.

Due to the congested traffic, I had to pass on Spagos; otherwise, I would be in traffic all day. I decided to visit Santa Monica and take in the Pacific Ocean for a while, and I enjoyed it. After a few hours, I went back to my hotel, got some sleep and then returned my rental car.

After returning my rental car, I put my luggage on the shuttle and headed to the terminal to await my flight. I placed my two bags and briefcase in the luggage rack across from me. Shortly after the shuttle driver made a couple of stops, he reached another terminal and stopped once again to let other passengers off.

A man walked from the rear of the shuttle, grabbed my briefcase, and attempted to hastily get off the shuttle bus with my briefcase. Fortunately, I was sitting next to the door, and as the man was about to leave, I grabbed him by his belt buckle and told him to put my briefcase down. He slowly stepped back, placed my briefcase back where he got it, and got off the shuttle. Luckily, I never forgot what my high school football coach taught me: "Whenever you tackle a running back, always reach for the belt buckle on the running back's football uniform because he can't go anywhere without it." Thanks Coach!

Over the years, I have traveled to several different countries, and I have vast experience traveling. I refuse to be intimidated by anyone or anything. I wasn't about to allow anyone to take my bag from me before I departed the United States.

My two pieces of luggage and briefcase were packed, and I was ready to make the journey to Australia. First I had to clear Customs, which was no problem, and then I had to wait a couple of hours prior to the 14.5-hour flight from Los Angeles to Auckland, New Zealand, and on to Brisbane.

I met some of the Olympians in the airport prior to departing on Qantas Airlines. The flight was full and it was going to be a lot of fun. The only way to mentally prepare for a long airline flight is to stay busy by reading, writing, watching some of the movies, exercising as much as possible during the flight, and of course getting up and walking around.

When Qantas mentioned we were passing the International Dateline, I was proud of myself because this was going to be the longest journey in my life. I thought about my parents because this is something they should have had the opportunity to do in their lifetime; however, it was me, the next generation, doing it.

Traveling to Australia had always been a dream of mine. I was living my dream and was willing to go after it with all the vitality and gusto I had. After arriving in Auckland, New Zealand, I thought about conversations I had with one of my previous supervisors, who had traveled here en route to the South Pole for duty.

My first impression of Auckland was how beautiful it was and how wonderful the people were. I did a little souvenir shopping and exchanged money while at the airport. Then I had a bite to eat prior to getting back on the plane for the final leg of the trip to Brisbane. I was fired up because Australia was only a few hours away, and I would be arriving on September 2, 2001, two days before my birthday.

Qantas Airlines did a superb job flying, and we safely arrived in Brisbane. I immediately went to Customs, was cleared, and went to baggage claim to get my luggage. I reserved a limousine and the driver was holding a card with my name on it.

I was able to get the limo driver's attention, then headed to my hotel to check in. I arrived at the Marriott, checked in and headed to my room. Athletes from all over the world were staying at the Marriott because of its central location to downtown Brisbane.

My immediate impression of the Marriott staff was positive, and it remained that way throughout my stay. Brisbane is a beautiful city, and its citizens make it even more beautiful because they are very nice people. I had so much fun and received the best service and was invited to dinner by the locals. Australians love Americans, or 'Yanks" as they call us, and I enjoyed their country.

I toured the Kangaroo and Koala Bear Sanctuaries and went on a trip to the Rain Forest. I visited the Gold Coast and visited a surfer lifesaving club and discovered it's not a sport in Australia—it's a way of life.

My birthday celebration took place at Michael's, a wonderful restaurant on the Brisbane River, which runs parallel to downtown Brisbane. The owner of the restaurant gave me the best seat in the house and they catered to my every need. Happy birthday Paul, you are now an honorary Aussie!

Brisbane represented the second Goodwill Games I had attended; in 1996 I attended the Goodwill Games in Long Island, New York. Track and field events were held at Hostra University. The staff in New York did a great job with the games, and I knew Brisbane would be enjoyable as well, and it was.

This was Michael Johnson's last official track and field meet, which was great to see. Marion Jones was there, along with the rest of the international track and field community, and I met more people who explained how to position myself for a role in Olympic-related activities.

I would likely move into the international sporting arena prior to retiring from the Air Force or shortly thereafter. Over the years, I had grown accustomed to international travel after visiting Europe many times, the Caribbean, Canada, and Mexico. I have traveled to or visited fifty states, and some of our Territories and Possessions.

The Australian nightlife is a lot of fun and people are just wonderful. If I didn't live in the U.S., Australia would likely be my first choice for places to live. Thanks for making my stay wonderful.

The Goodwill Games ended on September 7, on my last

night in Brisbane. I went on one last tour of the city because I knew I would be departing for the U.S. the next morning. For me, going to the other side of the world was not too far to go to bring my dreams to fruition.

It's incumbent upon me to inspire all people to be willing to go after their dreams. Distance and traveling should never be an impediment to reaching one's dreams. Never ever give up on what you believe in because it's your vision, and since most people can't visualize your dream, that doesn't mean you should quit striving for it. Your vision is your vision and to me it's sacred and should be nurtured until you achieve exactly what you desire. Be willing to go after your dreams no matter the distance.

We should go after our dreams with the tenacity of a lion, with boldness. It amazes me sometimes, while having a conversation with people that have never served in the military, how quick they are to say people in the military don't work hard. How would they know unless they have served?

On occasion I have discussions with people and they say you didn't really serve in the military if you were not a combat soldier or been to the theater of war. I simply ask these people when did they serve, and inform them that military duty comes in all forms, and that one doesn't have to be a combat soldier to be considered military. It's my belief that people who have never served their country be required to serve at least two years so we can continue our discussions on service to country. Sitting on the sidelines stating what a person did or didn't do while in uniform is not as important as having served honorably.

ACTION PLAN #1

Have a No-Limits Approach to Success

WE ARE THE ONLY PEOPLE WHO CAN STOP US FROM ACHIEVING success. When we look in the mirror we are looking at the pilot for our flight to the next mission. Our success is located in a region in our world and only we know the flight plan to get to our destination. By cultivating a no-limits approach, we will arrive safely at our destination.

Please list five no-limit things you need to accomplish during your flight check, prior to taking off for your trip to success. Don't forget to check your manifest to ensure that you have the right passengers on your success team. Please fasten your safety belts and enjoy the ride.

1. _____

2. _____

3. _____

4. _____

5. _____

We can mutually agree that getting to the top is not going to be easy. To be successful, we must be focused, but more important, we have to take a no-limits approach to make our dreams come true.

When I initially pursued my dream of participating in the

Olympic movement, I had to conduct a lot of research. Then I contacted a lot of influential people in the Olympic movement, and last but not least, I had to make my presence felt by getting actively involved in the process. Volunteering opened up numerous opportunities for me and I met everyone on the United States Olympic Committee (USOC) and numerous Olympians.

When I looked in the mirror, I was looking at the pilot for my destination to Success Mountain. Traveling to Australia for the 2001 Goodwill Games played a major role in me being selected to work with the Washington/Baltimore 2012 Olympic Coalition because they observed my level of commitment (no-limits perspective) towards the Olympic Movement. No one can stop you from achieving success except you. Trust yourself.

ACTION PLAN #2

Items to Include on Our Trip to Success

WHEN WE BEGIN PACKING OUR LUGGAGE FOR OUR TRIP TO success, we should include an abundance of enthusiasm. Enthusiasm will provide an uplifting experience for the passengers and ourselves on this journey. Don't leave home without enthusiasm, because we all need it. If we don't have enthusiasm, we will never be able to gain the speed we need to reach our cruising altitude. Enthusiasm is contagious and should be shared with other passengers on the journey.

The next important item we need to pack in our luggage is a joyful spirit. A joyful spirit can be viewed a mile away. People want to be around other positive people and are attracted to them. Sometimes people don't even know why they are drawn to positive people; they simply know they should be in their presence.

Our personalities can either make or break other peoples' spirit. It's incumbent upon us to treat other people with the respect and decency they so richly deserve. Be a catalyst for positive change by being a person who works to unite and bring people together.

We still have room for a few more important items to go into our luggage. Include some ethics in our professional and personal involvement with people. Take the flight path least traveled by being ethical in our pursuit of success to ensure we avoid the bumpy clouds so we won't encounter turbulence during our flight. The last item to include in our luggage is a barrel of fun. Please don't close your suitcases until you include some humor in your life, because it will sustain you during the journey.

Please write down seven additional items to pack in your luggage prior to departing for your trip to success. Only bring the items you know you will use on the trip.

1. _____

2. _____

3. _____

4. _____

5. _____

6. _____

7. _____

*"When you look in the mirror and can honestly say,
'I gave everything I had to achieve my dreams,'
then you are ready to succeed."*

—Paul Lawrence Vann

～ 11 ～

9/11 Changed America & Our Heroes are Fighting Valiantly

We all need a coat throughout our lives to protect us from the
unavoidable adversity that life invariably brings.
We need the loving, covering insulation to comfort our hearts
when we are challenged by the demands placed on us
as we make our way through the world.

—T.D. Jakes

ON THE MORNING OF SEPTEMBER 8, 2001, I BOARDED QANTAS
Airlines for my return flight back to the United States. I arrived
at the Brisbane Airport in sufficient time to relax and take in
the sights. I met athletes from Argentina, Brazil, Cuba, and the
United States. My flight took off at exactly 8:00 am as scheduled
and landed in Sydney, Australia for the transfer to the jumbo
jet flying to Los Angeles.

Again, and I repeat, in order to mentally prepare for a long
flight one must stay busy by reading, writing, watching movies
and exercising as much as possible during a 14.5-hour flight.
The return flight was great and the athletes on the plane were
fun because they let you hold their gold, silver or bronze medals they won in the Goodwill Games events.

The flight arrived in Los Angeles on September 10, 2001, at
exactly 8:20 am. I was originally scheduled to depart at 3:00
pm, but I immediately walked to my carrier and politely asked
if any flights departed sooner than 3:00 pm. I was informed

a flight would depart at 9:30 am and would have a two-hour layover in Pittsburgh, then arrive in Baltimore at 7:30 pm. I boarded the U.S. Airways aircraft and prepared for departure.

The flight to Pittsburgh was excellent, and even though I waited for two hours, I waited in the U.S. Airways Club room and relaxed away from the crowd. The customer service representatives informed me when to make my way to the departure gate, and I boarded the flight and headed to Baltimore.

I arrived in Baltimore, obtained my luggage, and waited for the parking shuttle to take me to my car. I departed the airport grounds at approximately 8:30 pm on the night of September 10th. It took me forty-five minutes to drive to my house in southern Maryland. Once I made it to bed that night, I was really tired from all of the traveling. September 10, 2001, was the last time I flew on a plane without concern for terrorist hijacking civilian aircraft; it was a memorable day of flying for me.

When I awakened on the morning of September 11, 2001, I was feeling under the weather so I made a decision to drive to the Naval National Medical Center (NNMC) in Bethesda, Maryland. September 11, 2001 was one of the most beautiful weather days of the year.

While driving to the NNMC, I turned on my radio and lo and behold! I thought I heard someone say, "One of the World Trade Center towers had been struck by an airplane." I turned my radio to another station and they reported the same thing. None of the reports made sense to me—something seemed amiss about a plane accidentally crashing into a building.

I was fifteen minutes away from the NNMC when I heard another report that a plane struck the Pentagon. I didn't understand what was happening, and was hoping I was still asleep and this was all just a dream. Unfortunately this was a living nightmare. I began to notice the traffic slowing to a complete stop on the I-495 North beltway.

I finally arrived at the NNMC and went to the Family

Practice Office, only to be told, "We are under a state of emergency and are not accepting any patients at this time." I was rocked from my foundation after being told all military facilities in the Washington, DC area were operating at threat level "Charlie," meaning the military was at full alert status.

Having been assigned at the Pentagon for over eleven years, I had a lot of friends that lost loved ones in the attack. In my county alone over forty people died as a result of the Pentagon attack. The Pentagon, World Trade Center, and Pennsylvania terrorist attacks were heinous acts. As a military officer, I knew the attack on the Pentagon would result in a declaration of war. Who in their right minds would attack the Pentagon—the very institution that makes decisions to send military personnel to war?

I told a friend that whoever committed this act of terrorism will look back and say we made a big mistake by attacking the Pentagon. Of course logic can't be used when talking about terrorists; however, after attending numerous military leadership schools, I knew that attacking the Pentagon would result in the attackers' own annihilation.

The traffic on I-495 South was terrible, but I finally made it home. What normally is a forty-five minute drive took over two hours on 9/11. I could see smoke coming from the Pentagon while driving home. I turned on the television and saw the horrific plane crash at the World Trade Center and the Pentagon, and it was life changing to say the least.

My heart goes out to the families of the victims of all of the terrorist attacks in America and around the world. I have lost so many family members that I am one of the elders in my family tree. God bless you all and may He add a blessing to your lives.

I almost decided to stay an extra day in Australia, but decided to fly back as originally planned. Had I stayed an extra day, I would not have made it back to the United States for a couple of weeks. I thought about how fortunate I was that the terrorists did not hijack planes on September 10th because I was flying all day from Los Angeles to Baltimore.

As many of us may recall, our cell phones and home phones were not working on 9/11 because phone lines were inundated. I was still sick because I didn't receive medical treatment on September 11th at the medical center.

Three days later, I went to a doctor and was prescribed medicine for my ailment and on the first evening I took the medication, I had a powerful dream. As I stated earlier, God gave me the gift of a dreamer but this was no ordinary dream.

The medication made me very sleepy, and then I started dreaming. I dreamt that something picked me up as if in the palms of a large hand and was taking me to God. In the dream my subconscious was telling me that if you see God you will die. I tried to wake up but I couldn't.

I assume whatever was holding me in the palm of its hand was a spirit; I don't know because it was a dream. Then all of a sudden the object in my dream that was supposed to be God said "I want you to get well." I have never had a dream like this before or after. What appeared in my dream as God looked like every color in the world—it was very colorful. All I can say is the medicine was powerful.

After waking up from my dream, I was screaming and laying in a pool of perspiration. It seemed as if someone had poured a bucket of water on me. The sheets in the bed were soaked, as well as my pajamas. I imagine after being sick for a week, and then being shocked by the terrorist attacks, stressed me out. It took me a couple of days to recover from my ailment, and then I was back to my old self.

Eventually, my phone was working again and my supervisor contacted me. He thought I was still in Australia. I was on leave from military duty and I requested a couple of additional days off just to recover from the jet lag. I received phone calls from people I had not heard from in fifteen to twenty years.

All of my friends knew I worked at the Pentagon. Some of my friends said they wouldn't talk long they just wanted to know I was doing all right. It is very reassuring to know that people genuinely care about you in times of travail.

I contacted all of my family members throughout the country to let them know I was doing fine and not to worry. It was time to get back to work, and I returned to my office; I was informed that the location of the terrorist attack at the Pentagon was the location of our old offices.

The National Guard Bureau moved out of the Pentagon while building renovations were taking place. Fortunately for us, we moved to a temporary office space until the renovations are completed.

Like everyone in America, I prayed because there was so much uncertainty just after the 9/11 terrorist attack. I was not afraid of anything before the attacks nor afterwards. My parents had both passed away and they would have been my primary concern were they still living. I am not afraid to die because it's a part of living.

I began to get back into my regular routine of working out in the gym, jogging, weightlifting, and everything else to relieve stress. I continued to arrive at the gym at 5:30 am in the mornings. I decided to jog past the Pentagon, and during my first morning workout I saw military Humvees and military police on guard around the Pentagon.

There aren't many people jogging at 5:30 am in the morning so it's very comfortable. When I jogged past the Pentagon for the first time after the attack, I stopped to take in what had happened on 9/11 and I noticed the construction workers near the side of the Pentagon where the attack took place. The men and women, who were mostly Hispanic, carried lunch pails and tool belts, and wore hard hats.

I jogged past what seemed liked hundreds of workers. I was proud to see the Hispanic community helping to rebuild the

Pentagon, which I consider to be my second home. I grew up and lived in North Carolina for over twenty-one years, and had been assigned to the Washington, DC metropolitan area for over eleven years, so in many ways I have lived a third of my life near the Nation's Capital.

The Hispanic construction workers made a tremendous contribution to America through their construction and electrical trade skills and talents. I salute the wonderful Hispanic people; thank you very much.

One of my good friends from Texas invited me to the Congressional Black Caucus (CBC) Annual Legislative Conference hosted in Washington, DC, in September 2001. The CBC was courageous to host the Annual Legislative Conference because there was so much uncertainty after the terrorist attacks on 9/11. In many ways, progressing ahead and moving on with our lives was important following the aftermath of the attack on our nation.

The CBC had a tough choice to make to proceed with its annual conference, but it made a wise decision to proceed. The CBC conference is an outstanding event, and throughout the course of the week, panel discussions were held by prominent Congressional leaders, culminating in the exchange of critical information such as the impact 9/11 would have on our lives in the future.

Oftentimes the difference in people receiving service in their communities is predicated on having accurate information to make a decision on safe communities, health, and medical decisions and policies we should consider that will help make our communities and country progress.

The highlight of the CBC weekend for me was being introduced to Ms. Coretta Scott King, widow of Dr. Martin Luther King, Jr. When I lived in Atlanta, I visited the King Center on a regular basis because I enjoyed discovering new things about Dr. King and his family. When my family members visited

Atlanta, I always included Dr. King's childhood home on my list of places to see because I admired his courage, intelligence, and persistence.

Former President William Jefferson Clinton was the keynote speaker at the CBC black tie dinner, and he was accompanied by Senator Hillary Rodham Clinton. All in all, the CBC transcends America because they understand inclusion. The CBC understands we all need each other to make America better in the future.

The events of 9/11 changed me because I had never seen anything so devastating in my entire life. I knew America would change and she did, and it seemed as though we were making a turn towards more unity in the United States. We had a right to be angry about the events that took place on 9/11, and we have a responsibility to bring the perpetrators to justice.

I want everyone to understand I was a military officer at the time the events of 9/11 occurred, and only by the grace of God, me and my comrades in arms didn't lose our lives that day. So 9/11 is a personal matter for me because the terrorists simply aimed and fired and didn't care who they killed on that fateful day. I love America, and my goal is to help her heal through my contributions to society and humanity.

America, we must be able to overcome adversity. We are doing a wonderful job of recovering from a full and direct frontal assault on our homeland. We have what it takes to be better and we are well on our way to healing in the process.

Like many people in America, 9/11 provided me with a new beginning. I sat down and conducted a self-assessment of where I had been, where I currently was, and where I wanted to be in the future. I know my parents wanted the best for all of their children, and they wanted us to have a better lifestyle than they had as children and as adults.

After completing the first part of my self-assessment, I came to the conclusion that I had come a long way from the poverty, lack of opportunity, and discrimination that was a way of life for my family, community, and country. In essence, each day of living is a tribute to the American Dream. Were I born in another country, there is no way I could have accomplished so much in such a short period of time. America is truly in a class by itself when it comes to its way of life and it takes patriots from all walks of life to maintain our freedom, liberty, and hope for a better America.

The second part of my self-assessment yielded results reflecting my goal to make a mark on society, and I was accomplishing my current goals because I was serving my country. Serving one's country is the ultimate undertaking, and one which acknowledges that as a volunteer in today's military, one could be called upon to give one's life for his or her country, as many of today's military troops are currently doing.

I was not a combat soldier; however, I am of the belief that at times the pen is mightier than the sword. I served my country with pride, dignity, and the tenacity required to move mountains and part the seas. I am very patriotic and would defend my country to the end. When you love what you are doing, you will never work another day in your life. I did not approach my military duty as work as much as I considered it fun, and I couldn't wait to get into the office each and every morning to help make America more secure than the preceding day, week, month, or year.

The third and final part of my self-assessment involved taking a critical assessment of my future. Would I stay in the military or would I retire after twenty years of service? This was not an easy choice for me; in fact, it was hard, so I prayed about it and asked that whatever decision I made was according to God's will.

🌱

I decided to retire with twenty years of service and cap an outstanding career for myself because I had already beaten the odds. I was not supposed to be where I was at this juncture of my life, much less as a military officer in the rank of Lieutenant Colonel. Many of my family and friends thought I was making a mistake by retiring; however, I knew it was time to transition to civilian life again.

My supervisor requested that I remain on duty for two years; however, I knew this would not work for me. When one has a calling, nothing should stand in the way of reaching your destiny. If I stood in the way of my destiny, I would be going against God, and I didn't want that to happen. Throughout my entire life, I have known what the right decision was for me, especially when it was an important professional or personal decision.

My supervisor understood my reason for wanting to retire. Throughout my military career I never married nor had children. For me, family and children weren't compatible for a military life because I didn't want to be killed on duty and my wife become a widow and my children grow up without a father. My objective after joining the military was to be available for my parents and siblings should they need my help financially or otherwise.

I patiently waited until the stop-loss (no separation or retirement) order was written by the Air Force before I could process my retirement orders. Once the Air Force lifted its stop-loss policy, I filed my retirement paperwork and October 31, 2002, was going to be my last day of military duty.

I had less than a year to retire and I did all I could to get on with my life after 9/11. It was important to stay busy because it took my mind off of the fear of another terrorist attack. The office building I worked in had twelve floors and the office I worked in was on the ninth floor. If we were attacked, it would be impossible to survive. I always kept in the back of my mind the possibilities of being attacked and what I would do to try to make it out safely.

ACTION PLAN #1

We Can All do Our Part to Help America Heal

ON SEPTEMBER 11, 2001, OUR COUNTRY EXPERIENCED A DEV-
ASTATING act of terrorism—it was horrific. 9/11 was a warning
sign for America and the rest of the free world. It was not only
one of the worst acts perpetrated on American soil, but also
against the entire world.

We can all help our country heal by continuing to pray and
meditate for one another. There is nothing we can do to bring
back our fellow Americans who were tragically killed on that
fateful day, but we can pray that their loved ones are continuing to heal.

It's also incumbent upon us all to pray for the safety of our
armed services personnel and their families. The War on
Terrorism is one of the toughest in recorded history. Young
men and women are putting it all on the line so our country
can maintain its liberty, freedom, way of life, and most importantly our hope for a better America.

Take some time to write down seven ways to help our country heal. I mentioned prayer and meditation, but I know there
is more we can do. After you write your list, discuss it with
your family, relatives, neighbors, and members of your church,
and help one another heal.

1. _____

2. _____

3. _____

4. _____

5. _____

6. _____

7. _____

Over the course of the summer I toured the United States providing motivational speeches to children of deployed service members. Oftentimes military children are forgotten in a time of war; please don't forget them because they also serve. When I think about my life and the fact that I grew up with both of my parents I couldn't image the pressure our military youth face on a daily basis. Loved ones left behind whether husband, wife, or guardian have a tremendous burden thinking about their loved ones on the frontlines in Iraq, Afghanistan and the rest of the world. Our military families deserve our respect and we should help them because they are making our country safer.

ACTION PLAN #2

Stay Motivated During Challenging Times

WITHOUT CHALLENGES WE WOULD NEVER KNOW HOW STRONG we are. The best way to overcome hurdles in life is to prepare for all situations, both good and bad.

When we are in the zone making great things happen, without fail something comes along and throws a wrench in our plans, projects, and dreams. Do not despair; chalk it up to a short-term setback and press forward with your primary objective to succeed at all costs.

Staying motivated throughout the course of our temporary setbacks will help us discover that success is just around the corner. Stay positive and don't listen to the negative conversations inside of you; they occasionally rear their heads, but we can deflect them simply by consistently reaffirming our goals. Challenging times are good times so let the good times roll.

Please list five ways you can stay motivated during challenging times and incorporate them into your success plan.

1. _____

2. _____

3. _____

4. _____

5. _____

Suggestions for Facing Challenges

Military personnel have incredible coping skills and we should never forget to leverage them when we are confronted with a difficult situation. We learned how to cope while in basic training and in our leadership and development schools. We are living in a fast paced society, since we understand this we simply need to take a couple of personal health days or leave to relieve the stress or tension we might be experiencing and sort out what we really need to accomplish in order to overcome our challenges.

Our military families and youth also need coping skills to deal with the deployment-related stress. We can overcome anything as long as we are willing to accept change; 9/11 represents the change we must address. I recommend meeting with family readiness and family support organizations at your duty stations or nearest reserve station and take advantage of the benefits to be derived from the resources in our communities.

～ 12 ～

The Final Military Salute

Peace of mind is wealth.
Peace of mind helps you live your life on your own terms,
in values of your own choosing,
so that every day your life grows richer and greater.
—Dennis Kimbro & Napoleon Hill

NEW YEAR'S 2002 CAME AND WENT, AND I ONLY HAD TEN months left on my military commitment prior to retiring. As Policy Branch Chief, I selected a civilian to assist with the transition of my pending retirement.

I was very proud of my branch's contribution to the Office of Policy and Liaison. No one wanted to work in the branch because the work was considered mundane compared to working on Capitol Hill issues. Nonetheless, the Policy Branch was in high demand because the National Guard Bureau knew we could produce positive results, and I am proud of everyone that worked for me and with me because it was very challenging.

A lot of my friends and family encouraged me to stick around for another tour of duty, and for promotion to full colonel. I knew sticking around was not part of God's plan for me, and I understood what my calling was, so I began pursuing it.

I attended an Air Force Career Planning and Management Workshop sponsored by the Air National Guard, and then I attended a Transition Assistance Program (TAP) at Bolling AFB. The Bolling TAP program consisted of pending retirees such as myself conducting career assessments focusing on what we really want to do for a living after the military. I thought about how much I enjoyed the speaker's bureau experience I had at Scott, AFB so I decided I wanted my second career to be fun and something I thoroughly enjoy doing.

An opportunity to participate in the Olympic movement presented itself in the spring of 2002. I was tracking Washington/Baltimore 2012 discussions and meetings pertaining to volunteer opportunities. The volunteer committee selected me to assist them in their bid to host the 2012 Olympics in the Nation's Capitol.

I accepted the Regional 2012 Coalitions offer, attended numerous meetings with them, and was a lead volunteer for the Baltimore Waterfront Festival, which also hosted a stopover for the Volvo Ocean (Around the World) Race. As a volunteer, I was responsible for providing festival attendees with information pertaining to Washington/Baltimore hosting the 2012 Olympic Games, as well as obtaining membership in support of the 2012 games in our region.

The Baltimore Waterfront Festival is great because the energy level is very high, and the city of Baltimore knows how to host big events. I was interviewed by one of the local television stations as well.

In June 2002, the Washington/Baltimore Regional 2012 Coalition hosted the Youth Day event throughout Washington and Baltimore. The event was a success, in large measure because the volunteers turned out in force.

I was the primary point of contact at George Mason University for the track and field events. I provided oversight for twelve Washington, DC-area Olympians and we hosted children from the entire metropolitan area at George Mason's track. America Online (AOL) also provided volunteers.

Youth Sports Day was very successful, and we handed out tee shirts and goody bags to numerous children in attendance. Some of the DC-area schools brought their entire track and field teams to the one-day event, and we held track competitions for all of the children. I was called upon to conduct a television interview with some of the local television stations, and this motivated me to improve my speaking skills even more.

The opportunity for accepting a position with one of the defense contractors was available; however, I knew I needed to do something in line with my goals. The TAP program really helped me sort out exactly what I wanted to do, so I set goals to achieve my dreams. I decided to become a professional speaker.

I joined Word Wrights Toastmasters Club in Fort Washington, Maryland so I could work on my speaking fundamentals. Then I joined the local chapter of the National Speakers Association in Washington, DC, so I could learn about the speaking profession from professional speakers. Toastmasters International really helped me focus in on specific areas of my speaking skills and abilities.

I accumulated over one hundred twenty days (four months) of vacation time, which I could either use or sell back to the government. I decided to use it. Instead of my retirement ceremony being held in October 1, was able to hold it on July 1, 2002.

All eight of my siblings attended my retirement ceremony, along with a host of close friends like Kimber Colton and her husband Jason, Brian Vigue and his wife Carla from Congressman Kennedy's office. My best friend Charles Brown and Amanda Bullard, former President of the Texas State Society, also attended my retirement ceremony.

My special guest was Ms. Meg Falk, who I worked with quite a bit pertaining to military funeral honors (MFH). I asked her to stand for a round of applause because she worked very hard after the Pentagon attack on 9/11, bringing her knowledge and wisdom to help surviving Pentagon families cope with the loss of their loved ones.

On 9/11 after arriving from the medical center, I turned on the television, and Meg was at a press conference updating our nation on the Pentagon attack and instructing family members what to do. Thanks for your service, Meg, I will always be honored to know you and I am proud of you.

Brigadier General Paul Kimmel hosted the ceremony for me, and I will always appreciate him for it. My retirement ceremony was attended by all of my immediate family members, friends, and staff. My retirement ceremony was held to let them know how much I cared for them and to encourage them to continue to pursue excellence because it's a part of their legacy. I almost cried when I thought about my parents, but I held it back because I knew they were looking down on their oldest son. I was very proud of what I had achieved in my life. My contribution to America came in the form of duty to country and I would not have done it any other way.

After the ceremony, we all feasted on the food provided, took a lot of pictures, hugged and shook hands, and wished each other well. Lieutenant General Daniel James, Director Air National Guard, was not able to host the ceremony because of his busy schedule. General James stopped by the conference room after my retirement to wish me well in my post military career pursuits. I saluted and thanked Lieutenant General James for his contributions to the National Guard, and I wished him continued success as well.

The only thing I wished for on the day of my retirement was that my parents were alive and attending my retirement ceremony, because they had more to do with me retiring than anyone at the retirement ceremony. I cannot stress enough the importance of family and its impact on America. Without our families, where would we all be? The likelihood is that we would not have progressed without our loved ones.

I also thought about all of the Vanns and Hawkinses, my ancestors that had come before me and blazed paths and trails before I was born. Somehow I know they had a lot to do with my success, because we never accomplish or achieve anything by ourselves. Without the love of my family, I would still be in my hometown looking for opportunity to come my way.

Most important, I know I have to give all praise to God through Jesus Christ because he set the course before me and challenged me to take up the cross and follow him. I view myself as a sheep being led by a shepherd. God gave me every opportunity I received; he used human beings to direct me to my destiny, so I thank all of my leadership, management, and subordinates alike for their outpouring of support over the years.

After the ceremony, all eight of my siblings drove back to North Carolina to their homes and families. I drove to my house and reflected on my twenty-year military career and came up with one sentence, "I had a magnificent career and I would not change a thing."

My future was bright and I planned on enjoying myself. The events of 9/11 changed my perspective on life, and I planned on making every minute count. I am blessed to have been born in the United States, and I don't take it for granted.

ACTION PLAN #1

We Can All Attain Success

OVER THE COURSE OF OUR MILITARY CAREERS OR DURING A career transition, we can all be assured we can be successful. Take a deep breath and reflect on the contributions you make to a grateful nation; it's a worthy calling to serve one's country.

All of the education, experience, training, networking, and hard work we invested will pay off. Rest assured all things are possible by virtue of the fact we live in the United States of America, the greatest country the world has ever known.

America provides opportunities and unlimited possibilities to succeed, not once but two to three times. It's up to us as to what we want to achieve in our lives. Reaching the top of our profession comes with a price—our time is the most valuable asset we have and the only thing we can't recoup, so make your precious time count.

Motivation is the key that will propel your plane and as you push forward on the achievement throttle you will gain lift. Our enthusiasm will provide us with the lift to accelerate to our cruising altitude and our commitment to living our dreams will ensure we reach success.

Please write down seven things you are going to do once you attain success. Will you consider another great job opportunity or will you reflect for a while?

1. _____

2. _____

3. _____

4. _____

5. _____

6. _____

7. _____

ACTION PLAN #2

Helping Other People

Throughout my career, I have always enjoyed volunteering for different committees because I knew I was making a difference in the lives of others. Whether it was starting Junior Achievement Programs at high schools, assisting the Red Cross at military hospitals, or Black History Month activities, I enjoyed being of service.

I never stopped volunteering for committees, and over the years I was an Air Force Academy Liaison Officer for the Washington DC metropolitan area and helped a number of high school students receive academic scholarships.

I believe we all need to give back, and I know many of us continue to give our time and resources to many worthy causes. I salute each and every one of you who have not abandoned the greatest gift of all, yourselves. Americans are strong because they give so freely; thank you for your service.

Please list ten volunteer activities you believe are worthwhile. Review and discuss them with your family, friends, and neighbors. Encourage everyone you know to make a difference in the lives of other people, and you will discover they have greatness on the inside of them.

1. _____

2. _____

3. _____

4. _____

5. _____

6. _____

7. _____

8. _____

9. _____

10. _____

*"Serving one's country indicates you want to
make America a better place to live."*

—Paul Lawrence Vann

～ 13 ～

A Life Filled with Motivation

Speaking —speaking well —is like a great dance involving your
audiences, your customers and the great minds of the ages.
You coordinate the many intricate steps of this dance,
the gathering of knowledge, the marketing,
learning to better touch the hearts and minds.

—Dottie Walters

AFTER MY RETIREMENT CEREMONY ENDED, I DROVE HOME
and relaxed a bit. Relaxation for me meant working with the
Washington/Baltimore Regional 2012 Coalition. I was becoming one of the top volunteers as we were preparing for the United
States Olympic Committee (USOC) site visit in Washington,
DC. Our meetings were very focused and detailed, and we
thoroughly covered every aspect of the pending USOC visit.

USOC committee members arrived in Washington, DC as
scheduled and stayed at the J.W. Marriott located in downtown
Washington. USOC members stayed in Washington the entire
weekend in order to visit every athletic venue and prospective
venue, such as the site for the Olympic Stadium in Washington
and surrounding communities. USOC members were very
professional and conducted a thorough site visit.

I learned that when it comes to international sporting events
such as the Olympic Games, you can only control things in
your span of responsibility, and you must live with the final
decision voted upon by the USOC, whether the decision is in
your favor or not.

Being a part of something special like the Olympic Games was a dream come true. Even though Washington/Baltimore was not selected to continue in the bidding process to host the 2012 Summer Olympics, I learned a lot from the experience and can always say I was a part of something very special.

New York is the United States representative city to host the 2012 Olympic Games, and after seeing how well they managed the 1996 Goodwill Games, they would be a great choice to host the games. Since Washington/Baltimore didn't receive the green light to continue their pursuit of the 2012 Olympics, I decided to focus my attention on other areas.

In June 2002, I attended Mr. George Fraser's Power Networking Conference in Cleveland, Ohio. It opened up my eyes to the unlimited possibilities of starting and managing a successful business through entrepreneurial networking. George is a tremendous man, and I conceived my business ideas by attending his annual networking conference. I encourage my colleagues to attend George's annual Power Networking Conference in Cleveland if you want to get to the next level of your greatness.

I attended a couple of local National Speakers Association (NSA) chapter meetings, and decided to attend the NSA annual convention in Orlando, Florida. In July 2002, I attended my first NSA convention and met all of the heavyweights in the professional speaking industry.

Prior to departing for the NSA Convention, I founded Laurel Wreath Communications Incorporated, a speaking, training, and consulting company, because I committed myself to living my dream of becoming a motivational speaker.

I met Zig Ziglar, one of my favorite speakers, and his lovely wife. I also met people like Mark Victor Hansen of *Chicken Soup for the Soul* fame; Stedman Graham, a fellow North Carolinian; Robert Allen; and Rosita Perez. Les Brown and his lovely daughter Ona Brown was there, and she is a speaker who will make a mark in the near future.

It was my fortune to speak with Dottie Walters of Speak and Grow Rich fame. She is someone I have a lot of respect and admiration for because she provides a lot of wisdom to the speaking industry, and she is to be applauded for it. Dottie conducted a seminar in Washington, DC, and it really inspired me to concentrate on the business of speaking. I will always thank her for it.

I learned a lot about professional speaking, and with full commitment, discipline, and passion, I believe I will make a mark in the speaking industry before my days are done. After leaving Orlando, I decided to launch out on my own in the speaking industry. So I arranged my own speaking engagements, as many speakers before me have done.

On September 9, 2002, I began my speaking career in Henderson, North Carolina at L.B. Yancey Elementary School—the school I attended as a child. The next day I spoke at Henderson Middle School, the junior high school I attended as a child, and finally I presented a 9/11 speech at Vance Senior High School, the school I graduated from.

Then I spoke at North Carolina Central University in Durham, North Carolina—my brother's college—followed by a speech at my alma mater, Shaw University in Raleigh, North Carolina. Chief Master Sergeant Valerie Benton, Command Chief Master Sergeant, Air National Guard, hired me to speak at the Enlisted Leadership Symposium in Houston, Texas, which was an outstanding venue.

I received a call from the National Guard Bureau requesting that I accept a program analyst position with the Family Program Office. I accepted the position because it would put me in a position to help military families and youth while continuing to speak on a part-time basis.

Family Programs assists military families with deployment-related matters as well as being a resource during peace time. Family Program Coordinators manage their programs at the

State and Wing level for the Army and Air National Guard, and currently support all military service members in their respective geographical areas.

Consultants such as Marci, Shirley, Pam, Mandi and me participated in an assessment that helped outline the requirements for Family Readiness coordinators throughout the United States, and it helped define efficiencies and areas of required improvement.

I was a program analyst for one and a half years prior to pursuing professional speaking on a full-time basis. I knew it was time for me to leave my contracting job because I knew my passion was speaking. It was an all or nothing decision for me, and it was wonderful because everything fell into place.

Reading is one of the primary requirements for speakers because we have to stay on the cutting edge of new management concepts, technical advances, and all things pertaining to our niche market.

It's very important for speakers to read books, because we need to continue learning about other people's lives in order to obtain more knowledge about the world around us. I was fortunate to read T.D. Jakes' book, *Maximize the Moment*, in which he states, "you are the most effective when you are operating in a there state of being."

What Bishop Jakes is saying is that the challenge is to live in such a way that you wake up not only the world but also yourself to the totality of your calling. After reading Brother Jakes' book I knew I had found my "there" and I have intensified my quest to be the best professional speaker I can be. I don't want to be like any other speaker in the world because we all have our special and unique gifts, talents, and abilities on the platform. Neither do I want to be like any other author; I simply want to be the best author I can be.

We owe it to ourselves to be the best we can be because we all have greatness on the inside of us and I have discovered my "there." What about you? I did not get here on my own; there were many people who provided encouragement and assistance along the way.

People who helped me find my "there" in the speaking business are people like Laverne Yates, Vera Turner, and Steve Siebold, because they listened to me and helped me gain more insight into the business of speaking. We all need people who are genuine in our lives and who will be there for us and be truthful and honest with us about our abilities. I thank each and every one of them for their assistance.

I was fortunate to attend the Bill Gove Speech Workshop in West Palm Beach, Florida. I learned everything I needed to learn about professional speaking. Steve Siebold and his wife Dawn conduct a superb speech workshop based on the principles of Bill Gove, the father of professional speaking. Without Steve's workshop, I would not be where I am today, and I can honestly say I am a better speaker for having attended.

I am an expert in motivation with an emphasis on military related issues, families, and youth. Of course leadership, diversity, and success, all translate to our armed services as well. I provide entertaining and thought-provoking speeches to my audiences. My objective as a speaker is to take my audiences behind the scenes so they can capture a synopsis of my actual experience in one of my speeches.

Over twenty years in the military provided me with a wealth of leadership knowledge and wisdom; thus leadership is one of my speaking topics. I also provide diversity training to Fortune 500 companies and associations because Mobil Chemical Company started me in this body of knowledge in 1988. My success strategies programs are very entertaining and have high-energy value. I love living my dream.

After making the all-important decision to pursue my professional speaking career, I returned to Henderson, North Carolina and spoke to students at K-12 schools to inspire them to understand the building blocks for their academic success. Then MasterCard International hired me to provide a motivational diversity speech to their corporate employees in New York.

As a motivational speaker, I have the responsibility to help people. During the summer of 2004, the National Military Family Association (NMFA) hired me to speak to over one thousand military youth in eleven cities and Guam. I provided motivational speeches to children of armed services personnel through a program called Operation Purple.

Ms. Lauren Rebeiz, Program Manager for Operation Purple stated, "Operation Purple is a first-of-its-kind youth program." In other words, they provided a platform for children from different military service families to discuss their unique concerns about their loved ones being deployed in support of war.

Campers attended free of charge, made new friends, had fun and discussed their futures. The Operation Purple tour allowed me an opportunity to learn and experience what military youth go through on a daily basis while their parents are fighting on the frontlines in Iraq and Afghanistan. I learned that our military youth also serve on the homefront providing support and encouragement to their parent or caregiver left behind as well as to their loved ones fighting in the War on Terrorism.

Military youth learned to face their fears on various team-building exercises such as ropes, rock climbing, sailing, horseback riding, and canoeing.

No one really knows what our military youth go through on a daily basis. I can say from personal experience that military youth are our leaders of today and many of them will be our leaders of tomorrow because they have courage, strong beliefs, and they share the hope our country needs during these challenging times. I am not worried about our younger generation being able to carry the torch for freedom, liberty, and hope for a better America; they are our shining beacons of light and will do just great.

The National Speakers Association (NSA), the leading organization for experts who speak professionally, accepted me as a professional member of the Association, and I couldn't be more pleased. I will continue to motivate, train, consult, and author books for years to come.

I never married or had children during my twenty years of duty in the military, and I planned on remaining single after retiring. A month after retiring, I met a lady by the name of Marites. One of her coworkers and friends introduced Marites and I and we began dating. My status as a bachelor ended after meeting Marites and we got married.

Marites' parents had twelve children, and I come from a family with nine children. We made an important decision to have a child, and on November 6, 2003, Marites and I became the proud parents of Paula Marie. So now we have our own family.

I was scheduled to attend the Bill Gove Speech Workshop in Fort Lauderdale, Florida on November 7, 2003, but providence interceded. Marites' doctor informed us she would deliver our baby on December 24, 2003, so we were confident December would be the month for delivery. On the evening of November 5, Marites told me she felt as if the baby had dropped.

Marites and I talked about early delivery but never realized it would happen. The next morning, I went to work and completed final plans for my trip to the Bill Gove Speech Workshop because I was scheduled to depart on November 7th. Marites called me on my cell phone to tell me I needed to come home to take her to the hospital to deliver our baby.

Ironically, I did not drive my car to the office that morning; I took the train and left my car at the metro station in Maryland. So I told Marites to be calm and call Odell, our neighbor who only lived a block away. Then I contacted him so he could drive

Marites to Malcolm Grow Medical Hospital at Andrews Air Force Base where her obstetrician was. Odell being the Army (Ret) soldier that he is, promptly drove Marites to Andrews AFB.

Meanwhile, I left the Crystal City Underground where I received Marites' call, and asked someone where the taxis were located. I ran towards a hotel; then all of a sudden a taxi was driving towards me so I raised my hand and he stopped. I explained to the taxi driver I needed to be driven to the metro to get my car because my wife was going to deliver our baby. He drove past downtown Washington as if it were not there; I arrived at the metro in ten minutes, a new land speed record.

I paid and thanked the taxi driver. I made it to my car and sped off and wouldn't you know it, all of a sudden I was in a traffic jam with no way out. I proceeded through the traffic and was driving aggressively, but I had a good excuse had I been stopped. I made it to Andrews AFB less than five minutes after Odell and Marites. After finding a place to park, I walked straight to the hospital room Marites was located in.

My wife's OB informed us Marites would be delivering the baby on November 6th but not at Malcolm Grow because they are not equipped to deliver premature babies. Her doctor arranged for an ambulance to deliver them to the Naval National Medical Center (NNMC) in Bethesda, Maryland, which is typically a forty-five minute drive from Andrews; however, it was almost time for the rush-hour traffic.

I informed the ambulance driver that I would be directly behind him all the way to the NNMC, and I was. We departed Andrews AFB at 2:45 pm and at 4:05 pm the ambulance team rushed Marites to the maternity ward. I parked my car and rushed to the ward. I entered Marites' room and nine people were standing there waiting to deliver our baby. At 4:15 Marites and I were informed she would be delivering the baby very soon, and we looked at each other and she looked a bit nervous, so I knew my role would be as coach and motivator.

The doctor and his team were set and ready to deliver, and they asked Marites if she wanted a painkiller. They asked her again, and then the doctor said, "Is this your final answer? Marites said, "No. My sister and mother did not elect pain killers and neither will I." Marites looked at me, and I and said, "If you don't take the painkiller, I will." Again she said, "No."

On November 6th at 4:45 pm, the doctors, nurses, specialist, and I all witnessed the delivery of a baby girl. Baby Vann and Marites were working in unison, mom was pushing, dad was encouraging mom to do her best as I breathed with her and the doctor took the forceps to bring our baby into the world. Baby Vann weighed four pounds, eleven ounces and she was long.

I gave my best speech to Marites because I needed to keep her motivated throughout the delivery and she thanked me for being strong throughout the process. I told her she was the strong one because she didn't elect to take the painkiller. Afterwards, she told me she wished she had taken it because it really hurt.

The nurses asked us what we were going to name the baby and I looked at Marites and she said Paula Marie. My name is Paul, my wife's name is Marites, and you get the picture.

Paula Marie is a very fitting name for our daughter because she is part mom and part dad. Paula Marie remained in the Neonatal Intensive Care Unit (NICU) for two weeks in order to help her develop a bit more before coming home. The excellent medical staff at NNMC informed us we could bring Paula Marie home with us for the first time during the week of Thanksgiving, 2003.

Marites and I have a lot to be thankful for. Marites and I are thankful for each other and our healthy and happy baby girl Paula Marie. I am a happy man and proud as a peacock to know God showed me favor after so many years of being single. I found my bride and I am a proud parent. My life continues to be filled with motivation because I have two people who love me unconditionally.

Although marriage is new to me, I am still discovering what it means to be a good husband to my wife and father to my child. My life has come full circle because marriage and parenting were the only two things I had never experienced before.

Now I understand and have a greater appreciation for what my parents were experiencing as husband and wife and parents, and I have even more respect for them because they were married forty-two years and were the parents of nine children.

Life after the military is very rewarding. Hopefully, you will have discovered some of the secrets to my success that you can adopt for your life. Whenever you decide to separate from the military or retire, simply look in your rearview mirror and you will see the positive difference you made in support of our country. Troops, families, and youth—we all serve a grateful nation. Continued excellence in all you do.

Each of us have important roles to play in our lives and we should continue to discover the best ways to continue Living on Higher Ground. I encourage everyone to continue to live your dreams and never give up on what you deserve in life. In the end we will all discover we deserve the very best in life and as long as we understand the power of motivation, we will reach our destiny and find happiness in our lives. Always believe in your dreams.

ACTION PLAN #1

Being the Best You Can Be

IT'S VERY IMPORTANT FOR EACH OF US TO GIVE OUR ALL BECAUSE none of us knows when we will be called home to be with the Lord. I encourage everyone to take an assessment of where they want to be five, ten, or fifteen years from now. Focus on what you love to do, where you want to live, and the people you want to be around.

We can do anything we want to do as long as we believe in ourselves and are not afraid to shoot for the moon. We are all stars and should let our lights shine every single day we have breath to breathe.

Don't take anything for granted—we owe it to ourselves to be the best we can be no matter what challenges we face. Make our lives count for a better tomorrow. Continue to make a difference in the lives of others, and make your life meaningful to you and the rest of the world. Go forth and be the best you can be.

Please write ten things you will do to support your efforts to be the best you can be. Follow through with these ten items and let them propel you to success.

1. _____

2. _____

3. _____

4. _____

5. _____

6. _____

7. _____

8. _____

9. _____

10. _____

ACTION PLAN #2

The Power of Motivation

THE POWER OF MOTIVATION PLACES US IN THE UNIQUE POSITION of being hope merchants. It's very important to spread hope for a better tomorrow because our children are observing our every move. We want children to see positive examples of what the world should be like. Motivation can cross the earth faster than a spaceship because people are the most important beings in the world.

Observe, look, and most importantly, listen to what people are saying and how they are saying it. When we are communicating, we are relaying messages that will have an impact on other people, places, or things. What and how we communicate represents the power of motivation.

Let's ensure we communicate positive messages that reach the eyes and ears of people who need reassurance in challenging and not so challenging times. We represent the power of motivation; thus, it's incumbent upon us to build people up, be encouraging, listen, share, and most importantly, help people. We are at our best when we help other people improve their status or condition in life, especially our military families and their children.

Please list seven things you can do to promote the power of motivation for our military troops and their families. Share your ideas with other people and encourage them to communicate positive messages.

1. _____

2. _____

3. _____

4. _____

5. _____

6. _____

7. _____

How do you define the power of motivation? Take a few minutes to think about the time someone attempted to help you. They likely were using the power of motivation to do it.

_____

_____

_____

Quick Order Form

Email orders: paul@paullawrencevann.com

Fax orders: 301-567-4954

Telephone orders: Call 1-800-476-8976 or 301-839-0948 and have your credit card ready.

Postal orders: Laurel Wreath Publishing, Paul Lawrence Vann, 938 Swan Creek Road E. #144, Fort Washington, MD 20744 USA.

Telephone: 240-476-8976.

Please send the following number of Books, CD, or Personal Journals:

_____ Book _____Personal Journal _____ CD

Please send more information on:

❏ Other books ❏ Speaking ❏ Seminar ❏ Training ❏ Consulting

Name: _____

Address: _____

City _____ State _____ Zip: _____

Telephone: _____

Email address: _____

Sales tax: Please add 5% for products shipped to Maryland addresses.

Shipping by air:
US: $5 for the first book or CD and $3 for each additional product.

International: $9 for the first book or CD $5 for each additional product (estimate).

Payment: ❏ Check

Credit card: ❏ Visa ❏ MasterCard ❏ AMEX ❏ Discover

Card number: _____

Name on card: _____

Exp. Date: _____ / _____

www.paullawrencevann.com

Laurel Wreath Communications Inc.

Services provided by Laurel Wreath Communications Inc. include:

Motivational Speaking
Keynotes, customized programs

Seminars
Highly Motivated Troops (HMT),
Family Issues, Youth Coping Skills

Training
Diversity, The Leader in You, Public Speaking Skills

Publishing
How to Self Publish Your First Book

Consulting
Military Expert

Contact personnel at Laurel Wreath Communications Inc.
to schedule your appointment
1-800-476-8976 or 301-839-0948.

I provide a free fifteen-minute consultation with you
and I look forward to working with you.

To obtain additional information about our services please
review our website at: www.paullawrencevann.com
or email us at: paul@paullawrencevann.com